John Dalton

A pilgrimage to the shrines of Saint Teresa de Jesus at Alba de Tormes and Avila

John Dalton

A pilgrimage to the shrines of Saint Teresa de Jesus at Alba de Tormes and Avila

ISBN/EAN: 9783741178610

Manufactured in Europe, USA, Canada, Australia, Japa

Cover: Foto ©Andreas Hilbeck / pixelio.de

Manufactured and distributed by brebook publishing software (www.brebook.com)

John Dalton

A pilgrimage to the shrines of Saint Teresa de Jesus at Alba de Tormes and Avila

A PILGRIMAGE

TO

THE SHRINES

OF

𝔖aint 𝔗eresa de 𝔍esus

AT

ALBA DE TORMES

AND

AVILA, &c.

BY

THE REV. CANON DALTON.

LONDON:
THE CATHOLIC PUBLISHING AND BOOKSELLING
COMPANY, LIMITED, (THOS. BOOKER, *Manager,*)
53, NEW BOND STREET, W.

1873.

NORWICH:
PRINTED AT THE MERCURY STEAM WORKS.

Ad Majorem Dei Gloriam.

PREFACE.

ERRATA.

At p. 23, line 15, read 1583 instead of 1853.
„ p. 25, line 19, read Classis instead of Classæ.
„ p. 42, line 5, read Henao instead of Hanao.

Mass in the very room in which St. Teresa was born, and of visiting the Convents of St. Joseph, and of the Incarnation, places so dear to all devout souls, and with which the history of the great Saint is so intimately connected.

How few, if any, English Priests have had such a privilege granted to them? How little is known by English Catholics of the glories of Avila; and of the stirring and most endearing associations that are bound up with the two Convents above-mentioned! It is true that Lady Herbert in her charming work entitled, "*Impressions of Spain in* 1866," gives us a few particulars respecting those Convents, *inside* the enclosures of which she had a "Special Papal permission" to enter. But it is to be regretted, that notwithstanding

Ad Majorem Dei Gloriam.

PREFACE.

While I was residing at St. Alban's College, Valladolid, in 1858, I should never have forgiven myself had I not *then* taken the opportunity of visiting the Shrine of St. Teresa at Alba de Tormes. When I was again sent to Spain, in the year 1866, by his Grace the Archbishop of Westminster, in order to collect subscriptions towards the erection of the proposed Cathedral in London, I visited Avila on my way to Madrid. Then it was that I had the happiness of saying Mass in the very room in which St. Teresa was born, and of visiting the Convents of St. Joseph, and of the Incarnation, places so dear to all devout souls, and with which the history of the great Saint is so intimately connected.

How few, if any, English Priests have had such a privilege granted to them? How little is known by English Catholics of the glories of Avila; and of the stirring and most endearing associations that are bound up with the two Convents above-mentioned! It is true that Lady Herbert in her charming work entitled, "*Impressions of Spain in* 1866," gives us a few particulars respecting those Convents, *inside* the enclosures of which she had a "Special Papal permission" to enter. But it is to be regretted, that notwithstanding

the golden opportunities which her Ladyship possessed
of furnishing her readers with *full particulars* of such sacred
places, her account of them is meagre and imperfect. There
is no necessity then, I hope, of any apology on my part in
endeavouring to supply what I consider is wanting in Lady
Herbert's account; though we are all indebted to her Ladyship for most interesting descriptions of the other Convents
of St. Teresa in Seville, Toledo, Salamanca, Valladolid, and
Burgos. But I have not confined myself to the Carmelite
Convents of Avila and Alba de Tormes. I have introduced
other matters which, I think, will be *new* to most English
readers, and to those especially who have never visited Spain.

Every year the name of the glorious Saint Teresa grows
more and more dear to devout Catholics. Almost every
year some new work in Spanish, French, or English, is published, throwing additional light on her wondrous Life, or
giving more correct and faithful translations of her writings.
Two very important works have appeared of late years, connected with her writings. The first is the splendid Spanish
Edition of all her works by Don Vicente de la Fuente, a
Professor in the University of Madrid. It is entitled:—
"Escritos de Santa Teresa, Añadidos è Ilustrados," por Don
Vicente de la Fuente "—(Madrid 1861-1862). I cannot.
speak too highly of this Edition. It is far superior to all
preceding ones. The learned Editor appears to have
taken the utmost pains to make it as complete and
perfect as possible. The Saint's Writings are placed in
chronological order; the defects, omissions, and mistakes
made in other editions, whether Spanish or French, are here
rectified. Don Vicente has also carefully compared the
printed text with the Saint's MSS. preserved in the *Escorial,*
the *Biblioteca Nacional* in Madrid, and several of the

Carmelite Convents in Spain. The notes and illustrations distributed throughout the whole of the Saint's different volumes by the Editor of this edition are exceedingly valuable, while his critical observations upon each of them are just and excellent. The first volume (Tomo Primero), contains (1), "The Saint's Life;" (2), "The Relations;" (3), "The Book of the Foundations;" (4), "The Constitutions;" (5), "Advices to her Nuns;" (6), "The Method of Visiting the Convents;" (7), "The Way of Perfection;" (8), "Conceptions of the Love of God, with some remarks on the Canticles of Solomon;" (9), "The Inner Fortress, or the Mansions;" (10), "Exclamations of the Soul to God, or Meditations;" (11), "Poetic Pieces;" (12), "Select Writings in Prose."

The following are their Chronological order and Titles in Spanish, as given by Don Vicente:—

Libro de su Vida*	1562
Constituciones Primitivas	1564
Camino de Perfeccion	1565
Conceptos de Amor Divino	1566
Exclamaciones	1569
Relaciones de su Vida á sus Directores	1571
Fundaciones	1573
Moradas	1577
Avisos	1580
Modo de Visitar los Conventos	1581

I have had the happiness of examining "The Autograph MSS. of the Saint's Life," "The Foundations," and "The Way of Perfection." The MS. of her life is preserved amongst the "relics" in the Escorial. It is written without hardly a single erasure, and in a fine, bold, masculine hand.

* This was called by the Saint—Libro de las Misericordias del Señor.

Her inkstand is shewn, but without the pen, which was *stolen* (I was told), a few years ago. "The Way of Perfection" is preserved in the Carmelite Convent at Valladolid, and "The Foundations" in the Escorial. In the "Biblioteca Nacional," Madrid, are also to be seen manuscript copies (very correct), of almost all the writings of the Saint.

The "Second Volume," (Tomo Segundo), includes the Saint's "Letters," and many which before had never been published. A valuable introduction is added, in which everything connected with them is said that can interest, instruct, and edify the reader. They are all arranged in chronological order, as far at least as can be ascertained, for many of them are written without any date. Notes and short biographical notices are appended to almost every letter; while references are given to "Letters" which appear in other previous Spanish editions. In 1860, I published a translation in one volume of several of the Saint's letters, but I regret that they were not arranged in chronological order. The Spanish edition from which I translated is the Madrid edition of 1798: this is considered not to be so very incorrect as some preceding ones. It consists of four thick volumes, 8vo., the first volume being illustrated by the valuable, though somewhat diffuse, notes of the illustrious Prelate, Don Juan de Palafox, Bishop of Osma. But as his Lordship did not live to complete his labours, the other volumes contain the Notes of a Carmelite Father, named Antonio de San José. According to the Bollandist, nearly all the Saint's Letters were written from about the year 1561 to the year 1582. (See "Preface" to English Translation, London, 1860.) This "second volume," so superior to all other editions, is indeed a treasure that cannot be too highly prized. To those who do not understand Spanish, their translation into French by Père Bouix, S.J., (Paris, 1861, 8 vols.,) gives us a clear idea of their beauty, purity of style, the deep interest that is thrown around them; the admirable vivacity and cheerfulness with which they are written; and the delightful outpourings of her noble soul which they display, whether directed to her Brothers, Sisters, Confessors, Bishops, Ladies of rank, Abbots, Priors, Nuncios, Rectors of Colleges, or to the Fathers of the illustrious Society of Jesus, several of whom were her learned Confessors, who, like Baltasar Alvarez, understood the true character of her method of prayer, not, however, to the exclusion of her Dominican Directors, in whom she put the fullest confidence.* Don Vicente, in his introduction to this volume, has said everything on the subject that can be desired. He has added seventeen letters never before published; the whole collection amounts to 408, the last letter having been written at Medina del Campo, on the 17th of September, 1582. I have given, in the Appendix, No. 1, a translation of two of the letters which the Saint addressed to her brother, Lorenzo de Cepeda; and another which she wrote to the Bishop of Avila, Alvaro de Mendoza, who was a great advocate and friend of the reform.

Another important work, which I cannot pass over in silence, is the Translation of St. Teresa's "Life," and the "Book of the Foundations," by David Lewis, Esq. (Burns, Oates, and Co., London, 1870-1871.) This gentleman is already known by his admirable and faithful translation of the "Works of St. John of the Cross," of which His Eminence, Cardinal Wiseman, once said to me—"These volumes are more like an *original* work than a translation."

* Especially F. Pedro Ibañez and Domingo Bañez. (See her "Life," chap. xxxviii.)

The same praise may be given to the two volumes above referred to. Considering the great advantages which this Spanish edition afforded Mr. Lewis, a new translation into English seemed called for, "because the original text has "been collated since the previous translations were made, "and also because those translations are excedingly scarce." (Preface xix.) Again, the translator makes the following modest remarks on the motives that induced him to undertake the translation:—"The present translation, the *fifth*, "has not been made because the former translations are in- "accurate or in any way unfaithful to the original; and he "who made it cannot refrain from saying, in his own defence, "that it was a task laid upon him by those whom he is bound "to obey, and one that he would never have undertaken of his "own will, partly because of the nature of the subjects of "which the Saint treats, *Mirabilibus super me*, and partly "because of the extreme difficulty of the work." (Preface xxi.) It is to be hoped most earnestly that Mr. Lewis will complete his difficult but important labours by translating the remainder of the Saint's writings, and even, if possible, a few volumes of her "Letters." The only thing which causes any regret with regard to these translations, is *the high price* which prevents so many from purchasing them, amongst a class of persons to whom they would be so interesting and instructive. Speaking of the Saint's works, Palafox uses these remarkable words: "No he visto hombre devoto de Santa Teresa, que "no sea espiritual. No he visto hombre espiritual, que si lee "sus obras no sea devotissimo de Santa Teresa." (Carta al Reverendissimo Padre Fray Diego de la Visitacion.) I have not known any one who was devout to Saint Teresa that did not become a spiritual man; nor have I met with any such person who has read her works that was not exceedingly devout to her. Luis de Leon also thus expresses his high opinion of St. Teresa's writings:—" The Holy Spirit has left "us, in her works, a most rare and admirable example : she " far outstrips the genius of many authors in the sublimity of " her subjects and the clearness and depth with which she " handles them. As to the purity of her diction, and the " elegance of her style (which are so pleasing to her readers) I " know no one in our language who can be compared with her. " Hence, as often as I read her works I cannot help admiring " them exceedingly—nay, in many parts it seems to me that " I hear, not a *woman* speaking, but the Holy Ghost himself; " for I am firmly persuaded that He often directed her pen, " and inspired her with thoughts and expressions," &c. (Preface to the Saint's " Life."*)

St. Teresa herself confirms the conviction, for she says: "As our Lord told me on one occasion, that " many of the things which I have written here were " not of my own invention, but that He, my heavenly " Master, told them to me." &c. How highly St. Francis of Sales speak of the Saint's writings, may be seen in his admirable Treatise on the "Love of God." M. Emery thus expresses his judgment of them :—" Les ouvrages " si recherchés, si estimés, si authentiquement approuvés " pendant sa vie, seront toujours un des plus riches trésors " de l'Eglise. Quelle longue chaîne ne formerions-nous pas, " si nous rassemblions tous les témoignages honorables qui " leur ont été rendus par les théologiens les plus célèbres et " les auteurs les moins suspects ? " (" L'Esprit de Sainte " Terese." Preface, xv.)

* For a short account of the works and life of *Fray Luis de Leon*, see Ticknor's "History of Spanish Literature." (Vol. II., chap. ix., p. 38. London, 1849.) His edition of the Saint's *Life*, was published in Salamanca in 1588 : it is not considered to be accurate.

Bishop Ullathorne, a great lover of St. Teresa, and one of the first friends I had to encourage me to continue the translation of her works, thus writes to me in one of his beautiful letters..........................." I hope you will be "able to continue the translations, which I am sure will do "great good to many souls. The *Mansions*, or the *Interior* "*Castle*, is a production that one might almost style 'inspired.' "Indeed, St. Teresa is eminently the Evangelist and Doctoress "of Mystical Theology. God gave her a particular faculty, "amongst her other sublime gifts, for translating her vast "internal experience of the mystic life into intelligible "language; and also of conveying what others might have "felt or known, but had never been able to express, by means "of ideas and illustrations, at once apposite and familiar. "The most remarkable feature in her writings, is that "vigorous, practical 'good sense' which pervade whatever "she says, or whatever she advises. How practical, for "instance, is the fourth chapter of the Seventh Mansion! "There is nothing vague or uncertain about what she says; "her language is of the most real, decided, and definite "character. That there are in her writings many things far "beyond the depth of almost all readers, is indeed most true. "But are there not things 'hard to be understood,' even in "the Holy Scriptures themselves? Alas! for *him* who reads "nothing but what he understands. Don't pay any attention "to foolish objections. How perfect will *they* become who "practice what they *do* understand, and who nourish their "faith with what they do *not* understand," &c.

Another jewel is also about to be added to St. Teresa's crown, already so resplendent. The Rev. Father H. J. Coleridge, S.J., has announced, as preparing for publication, "The Life and Letters of St. Teresa," (mainly founded on

Ribera's Life of the Saint, with the Letters inserted in their places.) Considering how admirably the zealous Father has edited "The Life and Letters of St. Francis Xavier," (2 vols., London, 1872-1873,) we may be certain that the Translation of Ribera's Life of the Saint, with the Letters inserted in chronological order, and each telling something of the Saint's virtues, will prove as interesting and edifying as the volumes connected with the "Life" of St. F. Xavier. We owe, indeed, a debt of gratitude to the *Society of Jesus*, for all that it has done in honour of St. Teresa, since the very first translation into English of her "Life" was published in 1611, at Antwerp, by "W. M.," of the "Society of Jesus." St. Teresa loved the *Society* as soon as she became acquainted with Father Padranos,* and ever since the *Society* has been devoted to St. Teresa. May we all love her more and more, and have the grace to imitate her virtues.

J. DALTON.

St. John's, Norwich, 1873.

---

* This Father, together with Father Bernardo Alvarez del Aguila, were sent, in 1555, by St. Francis Borgia, to found a house in Avila. This building is now the Bishop's Palace.

A Pilgrimage

TO

THE SHRINES OF ST. TERESA,

AT

Alba de Tormes and Avila, &c.

THE name of St. Teresa is now so familiar to English Catholics, and so great is the devotion of all devout souls to her, that the following narrative of a Pilgrimage to her holy shrines will, I trust, be acceptable to my readers. Often have I longed for the happiness and privilege of visiting Alba de Tormes and Avila, spots so dear and sacred not only in the eyes of all devout Spaniards, but in the estimation of foreigners also, who remember that the glorious Saint was born in Avila, and that she died at Alba, where her body is still preserved incorrupt in a magnificent shrine, while her heart and left arm may still be seen and venerated by the faithful.

This happiness, so long desired, was granted to me in the year 1859. With mine own eyes have I beheld the heart of a Seraph on earth—a heart that was miraculously pierced by an angel, and set on fire with divine love—a heart the very sight of which daily enkindles fresh ardour in the souls of the holy spouses of Christ, who keep watch around it. Even strangers who come from other lands afar off acknowledge, that in gazing devoutly upon that heart there seems to come forth from it a celestial odour—a sweet and sacred attraction, to choose *Him* for the God of their heart whom the great Saint loved so ardently, and served so long and so faithfully.

When residing in St. Alban's beautiful College at Valladolid, I should never have forgiven myself had I not then taken the opportunity of visiting Alba de Tormes. It was on another occasion that I had the happiness of visiting Avila, as I shall relate afterwards.

The Very Rev. Dr. Guest, the esteemed rector of the College, afforded me every facility for performing the journey, while the Rev. J. Mooney, then vice-rector of the Irish College in Salamanca, sent me a very kind invitation to spend the Easter holidays with him. Every necessary preparation having been completed, I left the College on Monday in Passion-week. On my way to Salamanca I passed through *Simancas, Tordesillas,* and *Medina del Campo.* As these places are illustrious in Spanish history, it may be interesting for many of my readers that I should say a few words about each of them, before I describe Salamanca and Alba de Tormes.

Simancas is the first town at which I arrived on leaving Valladolid, from which it is about two leagues distant. The Town and Castle originally belonged to the historic family of the Henriquez, who were the grand admirals of Castile. The Castle was taken from them by Ferdinand and Isabella, who, at the suggestion of Cardinal Ximenez, ordered it to be prepared for the reception of the national archives. But it was not until the reign of Philip II. that the archives were properly arranged and classified by Zurita, whom Philip employed for this purpose; while the two architects, Herrera and Berruguete, were directed to alter and adapt the building for the reception of the papers, documents, &c. These are exceedingly valuable, and are preserved with great care in different rooms. They are *now* accessible to scholars, who can easily obtain an order from Madrid to examine them as long and as often as they please. Formerly, however, these archives were guarded with the greatest jealousy. Robertson, Dr. Lingard, and other writers, both native and foreign, were unable to consult them with any satisfaction. But mere visitors can soon obtain permission from the "Archivero Mayor" to look over the building and inspect many of the curiosities. I was shown the Wills of Isabella, "the Catholic," and that of Charles V. Isabella's Will is signed by her, October 12th, 1504, Medina del Campo; while that of Charles V.—with a codicil—

was signed September the 9th, 1558, at Yuste.* (See Stirling's "Cloister Life of the Emperor Charles V.," London, 1853, p. 217.) I saw also the original deed of surrender at the capture of Granada by Ferdinand and Isabella, signed by Boabdil in Arabic characters, by which he agreed to quit Spain and live in Barbary. There are likewise many letters of Queen Elizabeth, Queen Mary, Philip II., Charles V., &c., besides historical documents of the greatest value, many of which have of late years been made known, to English scholars especially, by the valuable publications known as "Calendar of State Papers." At the restoration of Ferdinand VII., the royal archives—many of which had been plundered by the orders of Napoleon in 1810— were entrusted to the care of Senor Don Tomás Gonzalez, Canon of Plasencia. Though they were in great confusion and disorder, partly owing to the pillage of the French, and partly to the shameful neglect of the authorities, the worthy Canon soon put them in order. He immediately began to employ his leisure time for the benefit of historical literature. He profited by the abundant materials which were at his disposal, to compile a most interesting account of the retirement of Charles V. at Yuste. He had prepared his manuscript for the press, when death brought his labours to a premature close. His

* Not San Yuste, or St. Yuste, or St. Justus—but simply Yuste, so called from a streamlet which winds round the Monastery.

books and papers fell into the hands of his brother Manuel, who had succeeded him as keeper of the archives. But by the revolution of La Granja, in 1836, Manuel being reduced almost to poverty, sold the MS. to the French Government for 4,000 francs. It was soon transferred to the "Archives des Affairs Estrangères," then under the direction of M. Mignet. For an account of its subsequent history I refer the reader to Stirling's " Preface " to the " Cloister Life of Charles V." already quoted. At Simancas, St. Francis Borgia founded, in 1555, a Noviciate for the Society, where he often retired himself to renew his fervour, and hold sweet converse with God. A most interesting account of it is given by Maestro Alvaro Cienfuegos, in his "Vida, Virtudes, y Milagros del Grande San Francisco de Borja." (Segunda impression, Madrid, 1717, cap. XIV., p. 240.)

Tordesillas was the next town I came to. It is about four leagues from Simancas, and is situated on an eminence from which there is a magnificent view over the country, while the river Duero flows beneath the walls towards Toro and Zamora. Over this river is a fine arched Gothic bridge, supposed to have been built in the time of Ferdinand and Isabella. The town itself is now a miserable place, though it contains a few fine Churches, and the magnificent Convent of *Santa Clara*, in which the mother of Charles V., Dona Juana, lived in

retirement for several years, and died there in
1535, having watched for 47 years, with jealous
insanity, the coffin of her handsome but worthless husband. (Ford's "Handbook for Spain,"
Vol. II., p. 562, Ed. 1855.) The Chaplain to
the Nuns used always to be very kind to the
students of St. Alban's College, at Valladolid,
whenever they passed through the town.

I was very pleased when I arrived at *Medina
del Campo*, which is only a short distance from
Tordesillas. This ancient and interesting town
was once the residence of Royalty: it is known
in history as the place where the illustrious
Isabella, "the Catholic," expired, November 26th,
1504. The ruins of the Castle in which she
died are still to be seen. I visited them with a
melancholy interest; and with a like sad feeling
I also gazed upon the ruins of the celebrated
College which once belonged to the Society of
Jesus, and of which *Baltazar Alvarez*[*] was
rector for many years, and one of St. Teresa's
most holy and experienced directors. It may be
truly said, that a great part of the town is almost
a mass of ruins, which once were magnificent
Churches, Monasteries, and Convents. The
population in the time of Isabella is said to have
been about 50,000, now it is not much more
than 4,000. The Gothic Church in the Square,
dedicated in honour of San Antolin, is worth

[*] See his "Life," in Spanish, by the Ven. Luis de la Puente, or as he is often improperly called, Louis du Pont, and Da Ponte. The French and English translations cannot be depended upon.

seeing, so also is the fine "Hospital," in which St. John of the Cross was, in his early days, accustomed to attend the sick with such admirable devotedness.

That, however, which afforded me the greatest pleasure was the visit I made to the Carmelite Convent, which was the "Second" founded by St. Teresa, in 1567.* Having with me a letter of recommendation to the Rev. Mother Prioress, given to me by the Chaplain of the Teresian Nuns at Valladolid, I was at once received with extreme kindness, particularly as the Prioress was informed in the letter that I had translated into English some of the works of the Saint. Most interesting was the conversation which I had at the "torno" (grate), where strangers can speak to the Nuns who are inside. Many were the enquiries made about England, the progress of religion there, the number of convents, &c. When I told them that there were two Convents of the Carmelite Order in Protestant England, that the religious observed strict enclosure, and were all animated with the cheerful spirit of their seraphic foundress and mother, O! how their hearts seemed to rejoice, and what fervent thanks they gave to our Lord.

The following morning I had the happiness of saying Mass for this holy Community; after breakfast, I spoke again to the Nuns. Most precious and dear were the relics connected with

* "Book of the Foundations," translated from the Spanish, by David Lewis. (Burns, Oates, and Co., London, 1871.)

St. Teresa, which the Rev. Mother Prioress now shewed me, viz., a large portion of the Saint's incorrupt flesh; several autograph letters; book of accounts in the Saint's own handwriting; her Breviary; part of a vestment embroidered by her, &c. The Nuns appeared to be greatly *amused* in beholding with what delight I kissed, again and again, all the various relics which were presented to me. Their *cheerfulness* was most delightful, no one could possibly be dull in their presence. St. Teresa's cheerfulness has indeed descended upon them, as well as upon all the Carmelites in Spain. The mother of St. John of the Cross lies buried in the cloister. Her name in religion was Maria de la Incarnacion. It was in Medina del Campo that St. Teresa first met with Father John of St. Mathias—who had been but lately ordained priest—afterwards known as John of the Cross. "I spoke to the Friar," (says the Saint,) "with whom I was greatly pleased, and "learnt from him that he wished to become a "Carthusian. I spoke to him then of my inten-"tion of founding a Monastery of Friars, and "pressed him to wait till our Lord gave us a " house, and I told him what great good it would "do, if he led a higher life, to continue in the "same order, and how much greater service he "would render to our Lord. He gave me a "promise on condition I made no long delay. "When I saw that I had *two* friars to begin "with,* I looked upon the work as done," &c. ("Foundation of Medina del Campo.")

With sentiments of gratitude for the kindness which I received from the Nuns and their worthy Chaplain, and recommending myself to their prayers, I left Medina and hastened on to Salamanca, where I arrived the following day.

Great was my joy in finding myself within the walls of this ancient and venerable, and once-renowned seat of learning. I proceeded immediately under the direction of a guide, to the Irish College, better known in Salamanca under the title of "Colegio Mayor del Arzobispo," so called from Fonseca, Archbishop of Seville, who founded the College in the fourteenth century. I need hardly mention that I was received by the respected vice-rector—the Rev. J. Mooney—with genuine Irish hospitality. I soon found myself at home, and had the pleasure of being introduced to the students, then only eight in number, who were studying their Divinity. They all seemed animated with the true Ecclesiastical spirit, and made many kind inquiries about the Scotch and English students at Valladolid. The College is exceedingly fine, and so also is the Church, though it was sadly injured by the French during the invasion. This is not, however, the College where, during the last century, Dr. Curtis, Dr.

* The two Friars were Fray Antonio and St. John of the Cross. The former was tall of stature and the latter small. The saint used playfully to say—"that she had a friar and a half."—*Fraile y Medio.*

Troy, Dr. Laffen, and Archbishop Murray were educated. The building is now in ruins. It was only in 1821 that the present College was given by the Spanish Government for the education of Irish students. The first endowment in Spain, for the Irish Missions, was made by Thomas White, Esq., of Clonmel, at Valladolid; but it was translated to Salamanca by Philip II., in 1592.

After dinner, the Rev. J. Mooney accompanied me round the City and showed me some of the principal buildings, churches, &c. But alas! how fallen is Salamanca from what it once was in olden times! If one can fancy what Oxford would be were Christ Church, Corpus, Merton, Oriel, All Souls, Brazen-nose, and St. Mary's, reduced to ruins, then some idea could be formed of the desolation which reigns in the western part of the City. The "French invaders" laid in the dust all that was so venerable and glorious in this once-renowned seat of the Muses. The Duke of Wellington thus speaks of their ravages, writing to the Government at home (June the 18th, 1812):—"The enemy "evacuated on the 16th leaving a garrison in "the fortifications which they have erected, "on the ruins of the Colleges and Convents "which they have demolished. It is impossible "to describe the joy of the people of the City "upon our entrance: they have now been "suffering more than three years, during which

"time the French, amongst other acts of violence
"and oppression, have destroyed 13 out of 25
"Convents, and 20 of 25 Colleges, which existed
"in this celebrated seat of learning." The Duke
writing again in 1813, says:—"I have received
"intelligence that the enemy have destroyed the
"remaining College, and other large buildings
"which were at Salamanca, in order to use the
"timber for firewood, &c." (Quoted by Ford—
Salamanca. Part II., p. 516.)

We visited a few of the existing Colleges and
public Buildings, and of course the University,
of which the façade is indeed magnificent. I
was introduced to the Rector and some of the
Professors, who were delighted at being informed
that I was engaged on a translation from the
German of Dr. Hefele's "Life of Cardinal
Ximenez."* The illustrious Prelate was once
a student in the University. The "Plaza
Mayor," the largest square in Spain, was the
next place we visited. Then passing along the
Calle de los Moros (Street of the Moors), a house
was pointed out to us, in which it is said
Cervantes lived for a long time. We likewise
visited the Palaces known under the names of
Casa de las Conchas, so called from the *shells*
projecting out of each stone: the *Casa de las
Salinas*, with its overhanging roof and gallery:
and also the *Palacio del Conde de Monterey*,

* Der Cardinal Ximenes, und die Kirchlichen Znstände Spaniens am Ende
des 15, und Anfange des 16, Jahrhunderts." (Tübingen, 1851.)

with its turrets and arcaded windows. The new
Cathedral and the old Cathedral below it deserved more time to examine their beauties than
we had at our disposal. In the latter are some
very ancient and historic tombs. We were
informed that the remains of the Poet *Luis de
Leon*, were, a short time before my arrival in
Salamanca, discovered in the ruins of the
"Agustinos Calzados:" we saw the spot where
they were found. I visited several booksellers'
shops, but could meet with nothing but rubbish
and French novels. One exception must be
made. I found in a shop a volume full of
curious and interesting matter connected with
the history of Salamanca, entitled—"Compendio
Historico de la Ciudad de Salamanca, &c.,
escrita por Don Bernardo Dorado." (Salamanca,
1768.) But to know what the illustrious City
was in all its glory and renown I refer my
readers to another work, entitled "Historia de
Salamanca," por Don Gil Gonzalez de Avila,
4to. (Salamanca, 1606.)

The next day my rev. and kind friend took
me to the Convent of the Carmelite Nuns. It is
outside the gate called Puerta de Villa Mayor.
The religious were sixteen in number, all of
whom seemed to be animated with the same
cheerful spirit that I observed in the Sisters at
Medina del Campo. They conversed with us for
some time at the grate, all our conversation being
more or less connected with St. Teresa. From

the grate can be observed a beautiful painting of our Saviour's "Descent from the Cross:" the tradition is, that the great Saint purchased it in Salamanca for her Sisters. Several valuable letters of hers were shown to us, beside many precious memorials of her during her residence in the Convent. We were not, of course, allowed to enter the enclosure. This building, however, is not the Convent originally fixed upon by St. Teresa when she came to Salamanca. It was *inside* the walls. It has long since been converted into a private dwelling. But as Mr. Mooney and myself were anxious to see it, the Nuns sent one of their servants to show us the way. We soon arrived at the house, and were at once admitted. It must originally have been a large building : a part of the corridor and garden still remain. Inside are several large rooms which, as the Saint informs us in the foundation of Salamanca, were before inhabited by students belonging to the University. These caused great fear to one of the Saint's companions, as she herself thus relates in an amusing way :—
" Early the next morning Mass was said there for the first time, and I sent for more Nuns who were to come from Medina del Campo. My companion and I were alone the night of *All Souls*. I have to tell you one thing, my Sisters, at which I am ready to laugh when I remember it—the fears of my companion, Mary of the Blessed Sacrament, a nun older than myself and

a great servant of God. The house was very large and rambling, with many garrets, and my companion could not get the students out of her thoughts, thinking that as they were so annoyed at having to quit the house some of them might still be hiding in it; they could very easily do so, for there was room enough. We shut ourselves up in a room wherein the straw was placed, *that* being the first thing I provided for the founding of the house, for with the straw we could not fail to have a bed. That night we slept upon it, covered by two blankets that had been lent us. . . . . . When my companion saw herself shut up in the room, she seemed somewhat at her ease about the students, though. she did nothing but look about her, first on this side and then on the other; still she was afraid, and Satan must have helped her to imagine dangers for the purpose of troubling me, for owing to the weakness of the heart from which I suffer, very little is enough to do it. I asked her why she was looking about, seeing that nobody could possibly come in? She replied, "Mother, I am thinking if I were to die now what you would do alone." I thought it would be a very disagreeable thing if it happened. It made me dwell on it for a moment, and even to be afraid; for though I am not afraid of dead bodies, they always cause a certain faintness of the heart even when I am not alone. And as the bells were tolling—(it being, as I said before, the Eve of *All Souls*)—

the devil took advantage of that to make us waste our thoughts upon trifles; when he sees we are not afraid of him, he searches for other means. I answered her, "Sister, when that "shall happen I will consider what I shall do;— "now let me go to sleep," * &c.

The Lady who showed us round the house, was most enthusiastic in her praises of St. Teresa, assuring us—apparently with the greatest sincerity—that she considered it both an honour and a happiness to be living in a house which once was inhabited by such a great Saint. The Nuns remained in the place only about three years, as the person to whom the house belonged was very hard to please. Indeed, he afterwards became so violent in his conduct, that the Saint assures us—"she did not know what to "do with him, and Satan urged him so that "he would not listen to reason: we, however, "had fulfilled our bargain with him; but it "was useless to tell him so." The house, too, was not healthy, being very damp and excessively cold. Another house was therefore hired, and with the owner of this she had a great deal of trouble also. After the Saint's death, the Nuns were obliged to leave it for reasons mentioned by Yepes. In the year 1604 they removed to the present Convent outside the gate "Villa Mayor," already mentioned. (See note by Mr. Lewis, p. 131.)

* "Foundation of Salamanca." (p. 126. Translation by D. Lewis, Lond., 1871.)

While I was enjoying my visit to the Carmelite Nuns, I did not forget the chief object of my Pilgrimage—viz., the Shrine of St. Teresa at Alba de Tormes. I therefore requested Mr. Mooney to introduce me to his Lordship, the Bishop of Salamanca, for whom I had a letter given to me by the Cardinal Archbishop of Burgos—Fernando de la Puente.* I was received with that kindness and affability which the Spanish Prelates and Clergy always show to strangers especially. Having explained to his Lordship my desire to visit the Carmelite Convent at Alba de Tormes, and to be allowed, if possible, to enter "the enclosure"—that so I might behold the cell in which St. Teresa died, and pray before the sacred shrine which contains her body, his Lordship replied—"that this was a favour granted only to few "persons; but that as His Eminence of Burgos "informed him I had translated several of "the Saint's Works, and had thereby promoted "great devotion to her in England, he would "write a letter for me to the Rev. Mother "Prioress at Alba de Tormes." This letter his Lordship sent to the College in a few hours, of which the following is a translation. It was an open letter.

* Before his translation to Burgos, His Eminence was Bishop of Salamanca. In his youth he was educated at Ushaw. He died a few years ago in Madrid.

Salamanca, April 25th, 1859.
To the Rev. Mother Prioress,
    Respected Señora.
    The bearer of this letter is an English Canon, who has translated several of the works of our Seraphic Doctoress into English. His name is Don Juan Dalton, vice-rector of the English College at Valladolid. I have read his letter of introduction to me from the Archbishop of Burgos, who informs me that the good Canon has endeavoured, by every possible means, to increase and propagate the glories of our great Saint in England. He is most anxious to venerate all the relics in your Convent, wherefore, considering the pious object he has in view, and how much he has done in honour of St. Teresa, he deserves a thousand thanks. Moreover, in order that he may gratify his piety and love for your holy Foundress, we hereby grant the said Canon Dalton power and permission to enter the Enclosure and visit the Shrine of the Saint, with the consent of your Reverence. We also allow the Chaplain to accompany him. The usual precautions will not be omitted. May our Lord preserve your Reverence many years.   ✠ Anastasio, Bishop of Salamanca.

Having written a letter of thanks to his Lordship, I left Salamanca with feelings of gratitude to the Vice-Rector of the Irish College for his kindness and hospitality towards me. He had on the previous day hired a mule and a guide to accompany me to Alba de Tormes. On our way, the old man pointed out to me the site of the battle of Salamanca, gained by Wellington over Marmont, in 1812. There are two knolls called the "Arapiles," from the small village of the same name, through which we passed.

My guide seemed a devout person, for when he came in sight of Alba, he began singing a

c

hymn in honour of St. Teresa. It was exactly
twelve o'clock when we reached the ancient
bridge, that leads directly into the town over
the river Tormes, which rises about two leagues
farther towards Avila, in a place called Tormellas.
The water of this river is very clear, and
abounds with fish. (See Ponz's Viage de
Espana: tom. xii., p. 259. Ed. Madrid, 1783.

Great was my joy on entering

ALBA DE TORMES.

Here St. Teresa died; here her incorrupt body
is still preserved; here, too, her heart may be
seen and venerated in the Church of the
Carmelites, and also her left arm. What treasures are these, what sacred objects so calculated
to enflame us with the fire of Divine love, and
to behold which I had so long prayed that such
a happiness might one day be granted to me!
St. Teresa obtained it for me.

Having paid my good guide for his trouble and
attention, I entered the first Inn (Posada) I came
to, and took some refreshment, which was not
very palatable, as it was cooked in Spanish style
with garlic, garbanzos,* &c. After I had finished
vespers, I visited the ruined Castle and Palace
of the Dukes of Alba. It was built in the
highest part of the town, from which there is a
magnificent view over the country, the Sierra
de Guadarra being visible in the distance.

* A kind of Spanish pea, very unsavory to English palates.

Antonio Ponz, who visited the Castle in 1788, gives an interesting description of it, as it then existed, in all its magnificence. ("Viage de Espana," tom. xii.) It was very large, strongly fortified, and appears to have been adorned inside with paintings and sculpture, a few traces of which are still to be seen on the walls. The remorseless French invaders, on their flight from the field of Salamanca, reduced the building to a mere shell, one fine tower alone remaining. The place, however, became almost sacred in my eyes, as the Duchess of Alba, in the time of St. Teresa, was a most devout lady. It was by her particular request that the Provincial of the Carmelites ordered the Saint when she arrived in a dying state at Medina del Campo, on her way to Avila, to go instead to Alba de Tormes and spend a few days with the Duchess, who was anxious to consult her on spiritual matters. The town itself is small, gradually rising on the side of a hill, above the river Tormes. I visited a few of the Churches, viz.: San Pedro, Santa Maria, San Miguel, and San Juan. The latter appears to be the oldest and most interesting. In one of the side chapels are four very curious tombs of knights, recumbent under beautiful canopies. Having satisfied my curiosity, I was now most anxious to find out the Carmelite Convent, and the house where the Chaplain lived. This was a very easy task—every one seemed to know the good padre, *Francisco Quintano*. He received

me most kindly; and after he had perused the
letter of introduction which I presented to his
Reverence from the Chaplain of the Carmelites,
in Valladolid, he assured me, "that he would do
"every thing in his power to promote the object
"of my visit," and he informed me, that lately a
Jesuit Father,* from Belgium, had visited the
Convent, with the object of examining some of
the autograph letters of St. Teresa, possessed by
the community; and, also, that during the
octave of the Saint's Feast (October 15th), the
number of devout souls who come from Madrid,
and indeed from all parts of Spain, is immense.
As it was now getting late, the Chaplain told me
he would show me the Church, with its precious
treasures, in the morning, and that I was to call
upon him at nine o'clock. Thanking him for
his kindness I returned to the inn, but could
not sleep for several reasons. I was excited at
the recollection of the happiness I was so soon
to enjoy—of beholding the heart of St. Teresa,
and of kneeling near the shrine which contains
her incorrupt body.

I arrived at the Chaplain's house exactly at
nine o'clock. As he saw I was most anxious to
visit the Church, he soon procured the keys from
the Sacristan. We entered as the Nuns were
singing the Office. Taking the holy water, we
knelt down on the pavement to adore the blessed

* Père Marcel Bouix, whose Translations of the Saint's Works into
French are so well known and prized. (Paris, 1857-1864.)

Sacrament. Slowly and devoutly we walked up the Church, until we arrived at the spot, on the Gospel side, where the body of St. Teresa was first interred. The grave seemed to be deep; it is now covered with an iron railing. Descending a few steps on the side of it, we entered a small oratory where Mass is frequently celebrated. Close to it, and extending inside the Convent, is the old Choir of the Community with its grating. Originally the Church extended no further than this spot; but towards the end of the eighteenth century* the Church was considerably enlarged and beautified by the pious liberality of Ferdinand VI. and his Queen Doña Barbara de Portugal. The *new* choir, such as it now exists, is on a level with the sanctuary, which rises several steps above the pavement of the nave, so that the religious have only to remove the curtain of the grille to have a view of the high altar, and the saint's shrine, placed above it. The Church itself is large and beautiful; there are several altars in different parts of it, and *three* sepulchres. Two are on the Epistle side, and the remaining one on the Gospel side, at the bottom of the Church. Those on the Epistle side are the tombs of Don Francisco Velasquez and his wife, Doña Teresa de Layz. † On the same side, and at a short

---

* About 1750 or 1760.

† St. Teresa has immortalised their memory in her " Foundation of the Monastery of Alba de Tormes," dedicated under the title of our " Lady of the Annunciation." Lady Herbert incorrectly styles it, of the *Incarnation*.

distance from them, lies the body of Don Simon Galarza, who was also a benefactor to the monastery. Both these tombs are in a good state of preservation. The other sepulchre is that of Don Juan de Ovalle, and Doña Juana de Ahumada, his wife. In the same monument reposes the body of their son, Gonzalvo de Ovalle, who, when he was about five years old, was raised to life by the prayers of St. Teresa, at Avila; and at the age of twenty-seven finished his days at Alba de Tormes, and died a most edifying death. He is represented weeping at the feet of his parents. The religious having finished their office, the Chaplain took me into the Sacristy, where he spoke to one of them, and informed her that I had come from Valladolid to venerate the relics of their Seraphic Foundress and Mother. He also told her that I had brought with me a letter for the Rev. Mother Prioress, written by the Bishop of Salamanca. The religious took the letter from me, and went with it to the Mother Prioress. She soon sent a kind answer back, granting me permission to venerate the heart and left arm of the Saint, adding, "that she could not see me to-day, but "hoped I should be able to say Mass for the Community at seven o'clock the following morning. This, of course, I consented to do with the greatest joy and delight.

After Mass the Chaplain put on his surplice and stole; a candle having been lighted, we proceeded to the Epistle side of the High Altar, when a door was unlocked, and the curtain drawn back; immediately I beheld in a recess in the wall the crystal case containing "*the left arm*" of the Saint. The flesh, by the light of the candle, seemed to be of a dark chocolate colour, and quite incorrupt. I perceived a kind of celestial odour coming from out the crystal case. The arm is in a bent position. A great deal of the flesh appeared to have been taken from the upper part of the arm; but from the elbow to the wrist, the flesh is untouched. About nine months after the Saint's death, the Provincial, Father Gratian, came to Alba, when her body was again examined in 1583. Ribera, Yepes,[*] and the "Acts of her Canonization," testify that her body was then found to be quite incorrupt, sending forth a most delicious odour, &c. Father Gratian cut off the *left hand* on this occasion, and in 1585 gave it to the Carmelites in Lisbon, where it still remains.

Before I speak of the Saint's heart, let us first hear the account St. Teresa herself gives of its having been miraculously pierced by the dart of an angel, in the Monastery of the Incarnation at Avila. "Our Lord was pleased," says the Saint, "that I should have at times a vision of this kind; I saw an angel close by me, on my left side, in bodily form. This I am not accustomed to see, unless very rarely. Though I have visions of

[*] "Vida de Santa Teresa." (Cap. xl.)

angels frequently, yet I see them only by an intellectual vision, such as I have spoken of before. It was our Lord's will that in this vision I should see the angel in this wise. He was not large, but small of stature, and most beautiful—his face burning, as if he were one of the highest angels, who seem to be all on fire; they must be these whom we call Cherubim. Their names they never tell me; but I see very well that there is in heaven so great a difference between one angel and another, and between these and the others, that I cannot explain it.

"I saw in his hand a long spear of gold, and at the iron's point there seemed to be a little fire. He appeared to me to be thrusting it at times into my heart, and to pierce my very entrails; when he drew it out, he seemed to draw them out also, and to leave me all on fire with a great love of God. The pain was so great, that it made me moan; and yet so surpassing was the sweetness of this excessive pain, that I could not wish to be rid of it. The soul is satisfied now with nothing less than God. The pain is not bodily, but spiritual, though the body has its share in it, even a large one. It is a caressing of love so sweet which now takes place between the Soul and God, that I pray God of His goodness to make him experience it who may think that I am lying," &c. (D. Lewis' Translation—*The Life*, pp. 237-238. London: Burns, Oates, and Co., 1870.)

The Bollandists* prove most clearly that the vision was not intellectual nor imaginary, but real, and that the wound made by the angel's dart was a *physical* one. The Doctors and Physicians who were examined at the time, when their testimonies and solemn oaths were published in Rome, in 1726, are all unanimous in asserting, that the wound was both physical and miraculous. The same is the belief of the Saint's two early Biographers, viz., Ribera and Diego de Yepes, while in the " Bull of the Saint's Canonization " this wound is distinctly mentioned as *real* and *miraculous*. Hence Pope Benedict XIII., at the humble and pressing request of the Carmelites of Spain and Italy, granted in 1728 an Office (and Mass also), to be said on the Feast, which was entitled, " Officium Transverberationis Cordis S. Teresiæ Virginis, Duplex Secundæ Classæ." The Feast comes on the 27th of August, and is now kept by the whole Carmelite order. Benedict XIV. also, who is so great an authority in this matter, informs us that most authentic and judicial proofs were collected at Rome, and approved and examined by learned Divines, so as to leave no doubt whatever of the nature of the miraculous event. (" De Béatificatione et Canoniz. Sanct.," Lib. iv., p. 111, cap. viii., num. 3.)

This is the heart to which the Chaplain now directed my devotion. The curtain was drawn

* Acta S. Teresiæ à Jesu. (Bruxelles, 1845. p. 321.)

aside, and the crystal case* was then seen in which reposed the sacred object of my longing desires. Tears of joy, mingled with feelings of awe and reverence, so overpowered me that I was unable to utter a word. Now was the hour, and here was the spot, so capable of inspiring me with noble and generous resolutions, to love more and more ardently the same Lord, whom the glorious St. Teresa loved with her whole heart and soul, till she died of love.

The *odour* coming from this heart is, indeed, celestial. It inspires one with the sweetest devotion; with deep love for God, and contempt for the world and creatures. I saw distinctly, by the kind assistance of the Chaplain, the wound extending horizontally, from side to side, across the upper portion of the heart. It is quite visible. But above all I clearly beheld, on the lips of the wound, which must have been deep, traces *of fire*, which confirm what the Saint says respecting the dart of the angel having at the point "a little fire." Never shall I forget the impression made upon me by such a spectacle. I could have gazed upon that "noble and loyal heart" for hours and hours. But how happy was I made in being allowed to gaze upon it at all, even for half an hour! It has been said by some eminent Spanish Physician, that the Saint's heart is the *largest* human heart ever

---

* The Bollandists give, at p. 320, a large plate representing the heart in the crystal case. But I have in my possession a far better one, given me by the Nuns at Alba.

known. It is not exactly certain *when, or by whom* it was taken from the body. It was probably some few years after the Saint's death, and a short time before the Bishop of Salamanca ordered a visitation of the body to be made in 1591. The Saint died in 1582.

Having satisfied my devotion to the full, and thanked the good Chaplain for his great kindness, I left the Church, but returned again in the afternoon. I could think of no one all the day but the great Lover of our dear Lord, the glorious St. Teresa. Nothing any more interested me in Alba de Tormes, but the Church and Convent of the Daughters of St. Teresa. One of the religious noticed me praying before the High Altar, and sent word that I was requested by the Rev. Mother Prioress to be ready to say Mass again for the Community the next morning at seven o'clock. To this request I consented at once. After Mass the Chaplain invited me to take a *cup* of chocolate with him. A cup is expressed by the Spanish words " una jixara." Coffee is but seldom used, except in large hotels. We soon finished our cup, with which we eat a small piece of dry but beautiful bread. The good Padre was very soon satisfied. He knew not, however, how hungry I was, nor what a breakfast must be to satisfy an English Canon. I looked at the *jixara* to see if I could discover a few drops more. The dear soul took the hint, and asked with extreme politeness, " If I would like

another cup?" To whom I instantly replied,
"Si, Señor, con mucho gozo," adding with
apparent timidity, "that another slice of bread
would add much to my comfort." It is unnecessary to say that the housekeeper soon brought
up a double quantity, of which we both partook.
Padre Quintano seemed a very intelligent
person. My broken Spanish appeared to amuse
him much. He thought English a most bar-
barous, rough, uncouth language. He asked
me to recite the "Padre Nuestro"—*The Our
Father*—in English for him. He tried to pronounce the words, Father, heaven, hallowed, but
completely failed, after repeated attempts. I
told him how much our holy faith was advancing
in England; how many of the Anglican Clergy
and Laity had embraced it; how many beautiful
Churches and Convents had been erected in
different parts; and above all, that two Carmelite
Monasteries existed in that far-off land,[*] and
that the religious belonging to them were all
animated with the true spirit of St. Teresa,
and that strict enclosure was observed. At
these words his countenance beamed with joy.
"Gracias, muchas gracias," (he fervently exclaimed) " à nuestro Señor, y nuestra Señora,
Maria Inmaculada, Madre de Dios." He always
thought and heard (he said) that good English
and Irish Catholics were far superior in many
points to Spaniards : he regretted the increasing

[*] The holy Community at KENSINGTON was not then in existence.

prevalence of indifference to religious duties amongst the *men* especially in his dear country; but was persuaded that the great mass of the people were sound to the heart, and attached to their religion, and that if a good Catholic Government could be permanently established —. But the bell rings! The servant knocks at the door, and the Padre cries aloud "Adelante" (come in). It appeared that the Rev. Mother Prioress had sent for the Chaplain. He apologised for being obliged to leave me alone for a few minutes, and putting on his "Sombrero" he departed. He soon returned with good news, and with a cheerful smiling face. The Rev. Mother had informed him—" that taking into consideration what the illustrious Bishop of Salamanca had said in my favour in a letter addressed to her, how much I loved their Seraphic Mother, and what I had done by the translation of her works to promote devotion to the dear Saint in his own country; and moreover, that having taken the advice and obtained the consent of the majority of the community, she had resolved to admit me inside the Enclosure, and show me all the spots consecrated to St. Teresa. He was allowed to accompany me, and that at ten o'clock the Community would be ready to receive us." How delighted I was when I heard those words may easily be imagined; so too was the Chaplain, for although he had been connected with the

Convent for more than two years, he was never allowed to enter *inside* but twice, and then it was only to give holy Viaticum to two of the Nuns who were dying.

Exactly as the clock struck ten we arrived at the gate, which was at once opened for us. As soon as we entered the Enclosure, the Chaplain introduced me to the Rev. Mother Prioress, to whom I addressed a few words. We then proceeded in silence along the Cloister, visiting the different places and various spots—all more or less connected with the Saint's history, and with events which occurred during the few last days of her life in the Convent. Then ascending a flight of steps, we entered the holy and beautiful Oratory, directly leading us to the very Shrine in which the body of St. Teresa reposes. This Oratory is truly magnificent. The pavement is of blue and white marble, the ceiling is painted in blue, mixed with gold, and all the walls are covered with rich tapestry, paintings, and relics. From the centre of the roof hang three silver lamps, which are always kept burning. All of us now received lighted candles; several of the religious joined us; a bell was rung by one of them, and the gate was unlocked, which for a time concealed the Shrine from our view. We entered, and saw ourselves at once in the immediate presence of the sacred object of our love and veneration. We all knelt down, and prayed in silence for some time. *That* scene will never

be forgotten by me. I cannot describe the
thoughts and feelings which then crowded into
my mind, and agitated my whole being. They
were too sacred and personal to be recorded.
The whole history of the glorious Saint was
represented before me as if in a beautiful picture,
and all the edifying details connected with her
precious death passed before me one by one. I
was interrupted in my thoughts and medita-
tion by the Rev. Mother rising up; and
touching the Shrine with her hand, she said,
"Madre, oies?" (Mother, dost thou hear?)
What affecting and affectionate words were
these![*] Did they not show me that the Rev.
Mother Prioress and all the religious present
were most anxious, that their Seraphic Mother
should hear *mine* and *their* prayers? Those
prayers were many. It gives me great consolation to think that as regards myself I have
every hope my prayers were heard, and that St.
Teresa obtained many graces and blessings for
me.

The present Shrine was a gift of Ferdinand VI.
and his Consort. The upper part of the urn is
of jasper, with two angels sculptured on the top,
facing each other: one holds a dart in his right
hand. The lower part seems to be of bronze.
The Duke of Alba was also a great benefactor to
the adornment of the Shrine. Within this urn

[*] The Nuns constantly address their Mother in these and similar expressions, as if the Saint was really alive.

is another of solid silver, which contains the precious body of the Saint. I was informed that there are four keys belonging to the interior urn, and three which unlock the exterior one. The two last examinations and visitations of the body took place in 1750, and again in the year 1760.* At the former the Saint's body was found quite incorrupt, and as flexible as if she were alive; it sent forth a heavenly odour that scented and impregnated every thing around; while the silk and other garments with which the body was clothed were filled and saturated with a kind of oil which flowed from her limbs; this oil had a most delicious smell. The *right foot*, however, was wanting. It is now venerated in Rome. The *left hand* had been cut off, and is now in Lisbon, as I have before mentioned. The left *arm* and heart are also separated from the body, and so are the left eye and part of the upper jaw. Several ribs are wanting, and here and there considerable portions of her flesh have been taken off, and also some of her fingers, which are now to be found as sacred relics in Rome, Paris, Brussels, Avila, and other places. I myself have the happiness of possessing a small portion of the Saint's flesh, taken from her left arm, and given me by the Bishop of Salamanca. The left foot is quite perfect, and so is the right eye. But what is much to be regretted, the head was

* The whole account is given in the Bollandists, to whom I refer the reader. "Acta S. Teresiæ," &c.

found divided from the trunk. This seems to
have been caused by the upper part of the neck
having been, some time or other, cut away for
certain reasons now unknown. The *mouth* was
so firmly closed that it seemed impossible to open
it. (See Ribera's "*Life of Saint Teresa,*" Lib. v.,
cap. 11.) When the body was last examined, in
1760, it was found to be in the same state as it
was in the preceding visitation. The "authentic" account is preserved amongst the
archives of the Convent. By a Decree of the
Chápter held at Pastrana, the Saint's body was
secretly removed to Avila in 1585, for reasons
which then appeared just and proper to the
ecclesiastical authorities, as well as to the Provincial, Padre Nicolás Doria, and other Fathers of
the Carmelite Order. Alvaro de Mendoza, who
was formerly Bishop of Avila, was most anxious
to have the Saint's body interred there, as he
had expressed a wish to be buried next to her.
It was accordingly taken there with the greatest
care and reverence; and it is unnecessary to
add, was received by the Bishop of Avila, the
Religious, and all the Citizens, with the most
unbounded joy and delight. But when the Duke
of Alba heard of all that had been done against
his will and knowledge, he was so angry that
he immediately sent off a messenger to Rome,
with a letter addressed to Pope Sixtus V., begging
of His Holiness to command the Provincial to
restore the Saint's body to Alba, whence it had

been taken without his permission, &c. His Holiness immediately complied with his request, and sent a brief, dated Rome, July X, 1586, directed to the Provincial, in which he was commanded to take the body back again to Alba without any delay. This was done accordingly. It was also ordered that Alba should always be the spot where the Saint's body should repose. " Pronunciavit Pontifex Albam perpetuam Teresianæ Corporis Sedem fore." (Ribera, *Vita S. Teresiæ*, Lib. v., cap. i.) See also "Vida de Santa Teresa de Jesus (por Fray Diego de Yepes, cap xli.)

Having now satisfied our devotion, we left the upper Oratory, and descending into the lower Cloister, we entered the *Cell* where the Saint had expired, Oct. 4th, 1582, in the arms of the Ven. Anne of St. Bartholemew. What joy I felt on this solemn occasion, in beholding myself in so sacred a spot—surrounded by the devoted daughters of St. Teresa! Here the pure soul of their Seraphic Mother fled to the embrace of the God whom she loved so ardently; here a multitude of angels were seen glittering with wonderful splendour, gathering round her bed just before she expired, as if waiting to accompany her to heaven; here the remembrance of all the religious and innumerable devout souls, who for three centuries and more had invoked the sweet name of Teresa, in this House and Church—the recollection of all this was overpowering. The Reverend Mother Prioress pointed out to me the very spot, where the Saint's head rested when she expired. The Cell has been altered in many respects, from what it must have been when inhabited by Saint Teresa. Now it has the appearance of a beautiful little Oratory. It is covered with pictures and relics. It seems not to be above seven feet in length and five in breadth. The ceiling is very low. The account of the Saint's death is given both by Ribera and Yepes, who are the great authorities for all the most edifying facts recorded of a death so precious in the eyes of God and of men.* It is remarkable how frequently she expressed her gratitude to God when she was dying, for having made her a daughter of the Church. She seems to have foreseen the ravages which Protestantism was already beginning to make in Europe, and the consequent ruin of so many souls who would fall away from the Faith. She must have heard, too, how some Nuns and Monks, even in Spain, had been deluded and tainted with heretical opinions, &c. When the most blessed Sacrament was brought into her Cell, though during her illness she had been unable to move in her bed, yet she then rose up without any assistance and said, "O my Lord! the longed-for hour has

* A short account is given by Mr. D. Lewis, in his Preface to the Translation of the Saint's "Foundations," (xxii., London, 1871). I also have given another longer account in the "Preface" (xxix, &c.) to the Translation of the Saint's "Life," (London, 1851).

"come at last, now we shall see one another.
"O my Lord! it is time to go. Thy will be
"done. The hour of my departure from this
"exile is come, when my soul will be glad in
"Thee!" Then she added these remarkable
words, "En fin, Señor, soy hija de la Iglesia"—
But I am a Child of the Church. When Fray
Antonio asked her whether she wished to be
buried at Avila, or at Alba de Tormes, she seemed
displeased with the question, and answered, "Can
"I have anything of my own? Will they deny
"me here a little earth?" She often repeated
verses of the *Miserere*, commencing with the
words, "A sacrifice to God is an afflicted spirit,
"a contrite and humble heart, O God, thou wilt
"not despise. Cast me not away from Thy face,
"and take not Thy Holy Spirit from me, &c."
More interesting details are given by Abraham
Woodhead, in "The Second Part of the Life
"of the Holy Mother Teresa of Jesus, or the
"History of her Foundations," (Printed in the
year 1669, pp. 266-7, &c.) The Rev. Father
Bouix, S.J., also gives most edifying particulars
of her death in the *Appendix* to the French
translation of the Saint's "Foundations." (Paris,
1854 : "*Œuvres de Sainte Térèse.*")

Before I left the Convent, I thanked, as a
matter of course, the Rev. Mother Prioress for
her great kindness to me, and gave a small
donation to her in honour of St. Teresa, earnestly
recommending myself to the prayers of the holy

Community. I also thanked the good Chaplain for his kind attention to me, and then returned to the Inn. The next morning I went back to Salamanca by the diligence, and was again welcomed at the Irish College by my dear friend the Rev. Father Mooney, to whom I gave an account of my visit to Alba de Tormes. The next day I returned to St. Alban's College, at Valladolid, where the Very Rev. Dr. Guest, and all the students, as well as the Venerable Rector and Professors of the Scotch College, were delighted to see me once more amongst them. A few days after, I went to the Carmelite Convent, and there at the grate I told the Rev. Mother Prioress and the religious every particular connected with my Pilgrimage to the Shrine of St. Teresa at Alba.

Laus Deo.

AVILA.

In the year 1866, His Grace, the Archbishop of Westminster, appointed me, with the kind permission of my respected Bishop, Dr. Amherst, of Northampton, to undertake a journey to Spain, with the object of collecting funds for the erection in London of a Cathedral. His Grace being most anxious for my success, provided me with letters of recommendation to the Bishops and Archbishops of Spain; while at the same time I was to have the honour of presenting to Her Majesty Queen Isabella II. (when I should arrive in Madrid,) an autograph letter from His Grace, together with a most striking and beautiful print of His Eminence Cardinal Wiseman. When I arrived at Burgos, I called upon His Eminence the Cardinal Archbishop, who gave me a thousand reals (£10 sterling). The Canons of the Cathedral also contributed liberally; but I collected very little in the city from the Laity. The Archbishop kindly sent his Vicar-General to introduce me to the Lady Abbess of the Royal Convent of the "Huelgas,"* who received me

* So called, because built on the ground once occupied by "*Gardens of Recreation*" that belonged to Alonso VIII. (See "España Sagrada;" tom. xxvii: also Ponz. xii. 61.)

kindly, and gave me a small donation. Having
a few hours to spare, I found a person to show
me the way to the Carthusian Convent at
Miraflores, as I was most anxious to see the
glorious alabaster tomb, erected by Isabella, "the
Catholic," over the remains of her parents—
Juan II. and his second wife Isabella. The artist
was Maestro Gil, who completed the monument
in 1493. There is nothing like it in the whole
of Spain. No description that I could give can
convey more than the faintest idea of the impression produced upon my mind by this "Miracle
of Art," as I stood before it, vainly endeavouring
to master its details.* I had no time to visit the
Monastery of San Pedro de Cardeña, where the
Cid,† and his renowned charger, Babieca, were
buried, together with his wife Doña Ximena.
At the French invasion the tomb of the Cid was
violated, and brought to Burgos to decorate a
new promenade; but in 1826 the sepulchre was
taken back again to Cardeña with great pomp and
solemnity. But when all religious houses were
sequestered a few years later, his bones (it is said)
were put into a walnut tea-urn, and placed by
the civil authorities, under a glass case, in the
"Casa Consistorial," corresponding with our
Mansion House. There I saw them by paying a
few reals. But whether they *really* were the

* See "An Autumn Tour in Spain," by the Rev. R. Roberts. (London, 1860, p. 60.)
† His proper name is *Rodrigo Ruy Diaz de Vibar*, where he was born in 1066. (See "Pöema del Cid," and the "Chronica del Cid.")

bones of the Cid, or his Wife, or his Charger, seemed somewhat doubtful to my mind. F. Ozanam, in his "Pélérinage au Pays du Cid," (Paris, 1853, p. 24,) seems to have no suspicion on the matter, for he says "that thus the Cid's bones were saved from some *Touriste Anglais !*"

From Burgos I went on to Valladolid, and spent a few days in the dear old College,* at the kind invitation of the esteemed Rector. I collected day by day, in this city, from my friends who remembered me, several sums. The Archbishop and Clergy likewise contributed to the good work, and so also did the Rev. Dr. Guest and the students of St. Alban's, together with the Rector, Professors, and Students of the Scotch College. Indeed, every one was very kind to me. But the sum collected was not a large one, as the country was then passing through a *financial crisis*, which of course made money very scarce. My mission on the whole was a failure. The Papal Nuncio advised me, when I saw his Excellency in Madrid, to return to England as soon as convenient, and come back again at a more favourable time. This I did soon after I had the honour of being received by the King and Queen at the Palace. Her Majesty gave me £100, regretting much that circumstances prevented her from giving me much more. She spoke in the highest terms of Cardinal Wiseman, whom

* Both the English and Scotch Colleges in Valladolid belonged to the Jesuits before the suppression of the Society. The Rectors and Professors of both these Colleges are highly respected by all classes.

she styled "the honour and glory of Spain." From Valladolid I went on to Avila, where I called upon some of the Canons of the Cathedral, who gave me a dollar each. Unfortunately the Bishop was from home. The place seemed so wretchedly poor, that I had no heart to call upon any one else.

As I was anxious to go on to the Escorial, I remained in Avila part of two days only, but during this short period I was not idle. Everything around me spoke of St. Teresa. I seemed to be living in the XVI. century. The Jesuit Fathers, to whom the Saint says she was so much indebted, the learned Dominicans, the holy men who then lived in this city, which was honoured by the visits of St. John of the Cross, St. Peter of Alcantara, St. Francis Borgia, &c., the Augustinian Monastery,* where the Saint was sent for her education; and above all the Monasteries of the Incarnation and of St. Joseph, which are so dear and sacred in the eyes of all devout souls, and particularly so to the pious inhabitants of Avila;—these and many other persons and things came vividly before me, as I hastened from one object of interest to another in this beautiful and venerable old city;—probably the most unique specimen of a Castilian fortified town in Spain. The first place I visited was the noble mansion inhabited by St. Teresa's parents, now consisting

* " Ce Monastère existe de nos jours ; on voit, encore le Confessionnal òu Térèse se confessa quand elle etait pensionnaire ; il est près de la grille qui separe le chœur des religieuses de la nef de l'église." (Bouix.)

both of a Church and a Monastery, and including the very room in which the Saint was born, March 28th, 1515. Her father's name was Alfonso Sanchez de Cepeda, who married first Catalina del Peso y Hanao, by whom he had three children, one daughter and two sons. After the death of Catalina, he married Beatriz Davila y Ahumada, by whom he had nine children, seven boys and two girls. These were their names, according to Don Vicente de la Fuente *— Fernando, Rodrigo, Lorenzo, Antonio, Pedro, Jerónimo, Agustin, Teresa, and Juana. St. Teresa was probably baptized—not on the very day of her birth—but as Don Vicente I think proves from the testimony of a Nun in the Monastery of the Incarnation, on the 4th April, in the Church of St. John, near the Cathedral. I saw the font when visiting this fine old building. There is an inscription placed near it, stating the year and the day of the month in which the Saint was baptized. I regret now that I did not take a copy of this inscription. The Saint's name for twenty-eight years was Doña Teresa de Ahumada: but when she left the Monastery of the Incarnation to live in the new foundation of St. Joseph, she took the name of *Teresa de Jesus*. The account which she gives of her early years, in the first six chapters of her "Life," is written with the greatest candour, simplicity, and

* "Escritos de Santa Teresa," Añadidos 'e Ilustrados. Por Don Vicente de la Fuente. (Madrid, 1864. Tom. 1. P. 28.)

humility; the account of her parents, too, is most edifying and interesting. In a vision she saw them both in heaven, for she says in her "Life:"—"It seemed to me that I was taken up "into heaven; and the first persons whom I saw "there, were my Father and Mother." (Chap. xxxviii.)* I omit many things relating to the Saint, because they are mentioned either by herself, or by her Biographers. The room in which St. Teresa was born is now a beautiful Oratory, in which Mass is daily celebrated; it was converted into an Oratory in 1629, by the influence of the then Bishop of Avila, and by the co-operation of the Duke de Olivares, the celebrated [Minister of Philip IV. Above the altar is a fine statue of the Saint, who is represented as it were buried in an ocean of grief and sadness, as she beholds our Lord covered with wounds. There are several paintings hung round the walls, representing some of the principal events in the wondrous life of the Saint. Here also are preserved with greatest veneration—(1) a finger of her right hand; (2) her rosary; (3) one of her sandals; (4) her walking-stick,† &c. These I had the happiness of beholding. Lamps burn in this sacred place day and night. The monastery and the church are very beautiful, tho' alas! only three secularised

* See Note A. in the Appendix to Tom. I of F. Bouix, S. J., "Sur la Famille de Sainte Térèse." ("Vie de Sainte Térèse." Paris, 1857.)

† "Le bâton dont elle se servait dans ses voyages." (Bouix.

Fathers inhabit the house, and part even of this has been taken away from them. The spot where stood the orchard in which the Saint and her brother Rodrigo de Cepeda* used to build hermitages,—"by piling up stones one on "the other which fell down immediately"—is still pointed out. In the Cloister is a remarkable fresco-painting, representing different scenes in the lives of St. Teresa and St. John of the Cross. One vividly recalled to my mind how St. Teresa and her brother—(mentioned above)—set out from their parents home, " to go together to the "country of the Moors, begging our way for the "love of God, that we might be there beheaded," and how they were met after they had crossed a bridge on the road leading to Salamanca by one of their uncles, who brought them back to their distracted parents, that had been seeking for them all over the city. The figure of the Saint is radiant with beauty, innocence, and divine love.

My next visit was to the "Monastery of the Incarnation," outside the walls. Unfortunately, I had no letter of introduction to the Rev. Mother Prioress. But I ventured to ask at the grate " if an English Priest might be allowed to "see the Church, and to venerate some of the " relics of the glorious Saint Teresa?" In a short time the Rev. Mother herself most kindly came

* He was four years older than the Saint. He afterwards served as a soldier in South America, and was drowned in the River de la Plata.

and spoke to me through the grate. I soon made myself understood. When I told her that I had come from London to collect the alms of the faithful towards the erection of a large Cathedral in memory of Cardinal Wiseman, who was himself a Spaniard, and that the illustrious Archbishop of Westminster had given me "Letters of Introduction" to Her Majesty the Queen, and to the Cardinals and Archbishops of Spain, &c., the Rev. Mother Prioress seemed very pleased, and said she hoped I would say Mass for the Community in the morning before I left for Madrid. She then showed me most of the relics of the Saint, and other treasures. One especially was extremely interesting, viz., a crucifix carved in wood, and enclosed in a curious little box with folding doors, which the dear Saint always carried with her in her journeys, and which was placed on the altar when Mass used to be said. I also saw some of her letters, together with a few written by St. John of the Cross, and a likeness of the Saint, which the Prioress considered to be a very good one. It was not the one which was painted in the Saint's lifetime by Juan de la Miseria, and which she said was "very ugly" when shown to her.[*]

When I said Mass the morning I left I was told that the "Chalice" I used was the very

[*] Lady Herbert, in her interesting volume entitled "Impressions of Spain, in 1866," gives an engraving of this painting, at p. 166. The original was seen by her Ladyship in the Carmelite Convent at Seville.

same with which St. John of the Cross was accustomed to offer up the Adorable Sacrifice when he was Confessor to the Nuns. After Mass I was shown over the Church, which is indeed large and most beautiful. Both the Church and the Monastery are full of Memorials of the Saint, that fill our mind with the sweetest recollections. Though I was not allowed to enter *inside* the latter, yet the Rev. Mother Prioress told me many of the extraordinary favours which our Lord bestowed upon St. Teresa, in various parts of the House. She entered the Monastery,* Nov. 2nd, 1533, in the 18th year of her age; she made her profession here Nov. 2nd, 1536; here she had several wonderful visions of which she speaks in Chap. xxvii. of her "Life;" here her heart was miraculously pierced by the dart of an Angel; here she, and St. John of the Cross, when speaking of the Most Blessed Trinity, were both elevated above the ground in an ecstacy, and the chairs, too, on which they were sitting, were raised at the same time; here Father Francis Borgia (Borja) came to visit the Saint, in order that she might consult him on the state of her soul, and give him some account of her way of prayer: here our Lord first inspired the Saint with a desire to undertake the reform of the Carmelite Order, which had then fallen away from its primitive

---

* It was founded in 1513 by the pious liberality of Elvina de Medina.

fervour.* Here likewise she had that fearful vision of hell, of which the Saint gives so vivid a description in the xxxii. Chapter of her "Life." This vision was followed "by strong impulses to do good to Souls;" and soon after, our Lord *commanded* her to commence the reform with all her strength, promising her at the same time "that He would be greatly served in the new "Convent, that it should be called by the name of "St. Joseph, and that He Himself would guard it "at one gate, and His Mother at the other," &c. When I thought of all these things, I cannot describe the feelings which I experienced as I gazed on such a Monastery.† The whole building is "large and pleasant:" it is in a beautiful situation, lying amidst the verdant "Vega" that surrounds part of the walls. Lady Herbert, who had the privilege of entering the *Enclosure*, tells us that "the Cloisters are magnificent, with a spacious garden and orchard, watered by a clear quick-flowing stream." (P. 234—Avila.)

Thanking Rev. Mother for her great kindness, and recommending myself to the Prayers of the Community, I went to the Convent of St. Joseph, which is situated *inside* the walls, at the north side of the city. Upon this house I gazed with intense interest, because here stood before

---

* The Saint mentions in the xxxii. Chapter of her "Life" what were the relaxations which had crept into the Monastery of the Incarnation.

† The Bollandists give two plates of the Monastery—an exterior and interior view.

me the "first foundation" of the Reform, which
had cost the Saint so much trouble and so many
afflictions, all of which she overcame with such
wondrous fortitude, patience, and perseverance—
notwithstanding the innumerable difficulties by
which the devil endeavoured to baffle her exer-
tions, and damp her ardour and zeal for the glory
of God and the good of souls. The Convent
seems small outside. I had the pleasure of
speaking to the Rev. Mother, telling her I was
a Priest, and that I had just come from the
Monastery of Incarnation, &c. She seemed
pleased at what I said, and informed me—" that
" an English Lady (Lady Herbert) had lately been
"visiting both the Convents, and that she was
" exceedingly devoted to their Seraphic Mother."
She also said, that now and then some of the
Students from the English College at Valladolid
called at tho Convent, and venerated the relics of
the Saint. I replied that I hoped she would
confer the same great favour upon *me* also, and
that I might be allowed to see the Church. She
at once desired the Sacristan to show it to
me, observing that it is now much larger
than it was at the time of the foundation. The
Church contains two interesting tombs—one is
that of Don Alvaro de Mendoza, who was Bishop
of Avila, and afterwards of Palencia. Several
letters of the Saint are addressed to this holy
Prelate, who was so devoted to the Carmelite
Order, and such a great friend of St. Teresa—of

whom she speaks in the highest terms of praise.
In his will he expressly desired to be buried in
this Church, hoping to be laid near the tomb of
the Saint. The Monument is placed near the
High-altar, on the Epistle side, opposite to the
Choir of the Nuns. His statue is of white marble,
and is supposed to be a good likeness. The other
tomb is that of St. Teresa's Brother, Lorenzo de
Cepeda. He left Spain for South America, in the
year 1540 ; and entering the army, he became
Captain-General of the Province of Quito. His
wife was Doña Maria de Fuentes y Guzman, by
whom he had seven children, one of whom,
"Teresita," was adopted by St. Teresa, and
admitted as a Novice into St. Joseph's Convent,
where she edified the whole Community by her
extraordinary sanctity. There she made her
Profession—after the death of the Saint—in the
year 1582.* After I had seen everything in the
Church, the Rev. Mother Prioress showed me
most of the relics connected with St. Teresa—
viz., her *jug and cup;* her musical instruments ;
her leathern girdle: her discipline, and a cloth
stained with her blood, besides a bone of her
neck, and some of her letters and books—one of
which interested me much, as it was marked
with notes and observations written in the
Saint's handwriting ; I understood the Rev.

* Father Bouix gives a very interesting account of Lorenzo de Cepeda and his wife and family, in a note to his Translation of the Saint's Life. (Tom. 1, page 477.)

Mother to say—that the Book was by St. Gregory. I also saw a MS. copy of the "*Foundations.*" Several other memorials of the Saint I was prevented from seeing, because they were *inside* the Enclosure. But Lady Herbert saw them—viz., "The Saint's cell, now converted "into an Oratory; her, bed; her chair; her "clothes; and the coffin in which her body "was placed before it was removed to Alba." (Page 231.)

It is unnecessary here to repeat all the troubles, trials, and opposition which the Saint had to endure in the foundation of this Monastery. They are related in her "Life." (See especially Chapters xxxv. and xxxvi.) But our Lord helped her and consoled her amidst all her difficulties. "I am often lost in wonder," she says, "when I consider and see the special help "which His Majesty gave me towards the esta- "blishment of this little Cell of God—for such I "believe it to be—the lodging wherein His "Majesty delights; for once, when I was in "prayer, He told me that this house was the "paradise of His delight."

At last, everything having been settled, the Monastery was founded on the Feast of St. Bartholomew, 1562. The Father Provincial gave her permission to enter the house, and take some Nuns with her from the Monastery of the Incarnation. Their names were—Ana of St. John, Ana of all the Angels, Maria Isabel, and Isabel

of St. Paul. St. Teresa was then a simple Nun, determined to live under obedience to the Mother Prioress of the Convent—Ana of St. John. But the Community, beholding her wonderful virtues and capacity for governing others, begged the Bishop of Avila, and the Provincial of the Order, to compel the Saint to become the Prioress of the Community. The Saint thus speaks in her " Life :"—" It is the greatest consolation " to me to find myself amongst those who are so " detached. Their occupation is to learn how " they may advance in the service of God. Soli-
" tude is their delight; and the thought of being
" visited by any one, even of their nearest kindred,
" is a trial, unless it helps them to kindle more
" and more their love of the Bridegroom. Accord-
" ingly, none come to this house who do not aim at
" this ; otherwise they neither give nor receive
" any pleasure from their visits. Their conver-
" sation is of God only ; and so he whose con-
" versation is different, does not understand them,
" and they do not understand him." (Chap. xxxvi.) The Saint again speaks thus of these holy souls in the " Book of the Foundations." (Medina del Campo. Chap. i.) " I remained five years
" after its foundation in the house of St. Joseph's,
" Avila; and I believe, so far as I can see at pre-
" sent, that they were the most tranquil years of
" my life, the calm and rest of which my soul
" very often greatly misses. During that time
" certain young persons entered it as religious,

"whose years were not many, but whom the
"world, as it seemed, had already made its own,
"if we might judge of them by their outward
"manners and dress. Our Lord very quickly set
"them free from their vanities, drew them into
"his own house, and endowed them with a per-
"fection so great as to make me very much
"ashamed of myself. We were *thirteen* in num-
"ber, which is the number we had resolved never
"to exceed. I took my delight in souls so pure and
"holy, whose only anxiety was to praise and serve
"our Lord. His Majesty sent us every thing
"we had need of, without our asking for it; and
"whenever we were in want, which was very
"rarely, their joy was then the greater. I used
"to praise our Lord at the sight of virtues so
"high, especially for the disregard of every-
"thing but His service." *(Translation by Mr. Lewis.)*

The Convent seems to be held in high estimation by the devout citizens of Avila, who call the Nuns "Las Madres." I saw several of them through the grate, some of whom appeared to be very young. But all seemed to have inherited from their glorious foundress, her admirable cheerfulness—*Alegria grande*. When I told them that an excellent Life of St. Teresa had lately been published in England, composed by a religious, living in a Convent, near London—and not a Carmelite—and that it contained a preface admirably written by the present most zealous and

learned Archbishop of Westminster, and that
great devotion existed in England to their
Seraphic Mother, the Prioress and Nuns rejoiced
exceedingly. But I was at last, to my great
regret, obliged to take my leave of these holy
religious, and to bid "adieu" to the Monastery
of St. Joseph, to behold which I shall ever consider as a particular favour obtained for me by
St. Teresa. As the train for the Escorial left at
six o'clock, I found I had only a few hours
to see the City, the Cathedral, and some of
the Churches. The City walls seem to be
in a good state of preservation. They are
"40 feet high and 12 thick, defended by 88
towers," according to Ford.* The east end of the
Cathedral is let into the circumvallation, so that
the massive walls, flanked by the 88 towers, and
the Cathedral forming a part of the fortifications,
give the city a most mediæval appearance, and
seems to render it almost impregnable. Avila was
anciently called *Abula*, or *Abyla*, who is supposed to have been the wife of Hercules. The
City is said to have been founded 1660, B. C.!!
It was probably re-built about A.D. 1088, by Don
Ramon of Burgundy, son-in-law of Alonso VI.,
who employed two foreign engineers to erect the

---

* R. Ford, Esq., who died a few years ago, is well known as the author of "*A Hand Book for Travellers in Spain.*" It contains an immense mass of useful information, and displays great learning. But the work is disfigured by such a display of bigotry and prejudice against every thing "Catholic,"' that one is absolutely disgusted with the writer. What he says *against* St. Teresa under Avila, is unfit to be repeated, because too shocking to be read.

walls. The Cathedral was built about the year
1107. The western façade is splendid, of which
an excellent drawing is given by Lady Herbert,
in the work already quoted. (P. 226.) The interior is very fine, especially the glorious stained
glass windows, and the "Retablo" over the high
altar: it dates from the 15th century, and contains carvings by Juan de Borgoña, Pedro de
Berruguete, and Santos Cruz. (See O'Shea's
"Guide to Spain and Portugal." Part 1, page
29, London, 1869). Behind the *Capilla Mayor*
is the tomb of the learned Alfonso Tostado de
Madrigal, * Bishop of Avila in 1449; he died in
1455. His effigy, carved in alabaster, and clad
in his Pontifical robes, represents the learned
Prelate in the act of writing. The inscription
runs thus :—" Hic stupor est mundi, qui scibile
discutit omne." I afterwards paid a hasty visit
to the Churches of San Vicente, San Juan, San
Pedro, San Esteban, and San Salvador, all of
which seemed most interesting. Time did not
allow me to see the suppressed Dominican
Convent of "*Santo Tomas*," outside the city.
It contains the beautiful tomb of Prince Juan,
the only son of Ferdinand and Isabella, who died
at Salamanca in 1497, in the 19th year of his
age. It is a pity Avila is not more frequently
visited by travellers, as it contains even now so
many valuable and historic memorials of her past

* For a short biography of this famous Prelate, see Pulgar "Claros Varones de Castilla." (Madrid, 1789, tit. xxiv.)

glories. One Englishman, however, has at last done justice to the beautiful Churches and Cathedral of this once illustrious city, viz., Mr. G. Edmund Street, who published in 1865 a valuable work, entitled, "Some Account of "Gothic Architecture in Spain." (London: Murray, Albemarle Street.)

In Chapter VIII. Mr. Street gives a most interesting account of the Cathedral, Walls, Churches, with ground plans, &c. He concludes the chapter with these words: " It will be felt, " I think, that Avila is a city which ought on no " account to be left unseen in an architectural " tour in Spain. Fortunately, it is now as easy " of access as it was once difficult, for the " railway from Valladolid to Madrid, in order to " cross the Sierra de Guadarrama, makes a great " detour by Avila, and thence on to the Escorial," &c. (P. 179.)

Though I was delighted beyond expression with my visit to the City of St. Teresa, yet I felt as I was leaving in a sad desponding mood when I remembered, how I was unable to collect even a few pounds in a place that was once so rich and so flourishing. As I entered through the gate of San Vicente I prayed hard to the dear Saint that I might be successful in my " Begging "—and yet, as she cared so little for money herself, perhaps she was somewhat offended with me on seeing that *I* was so anxious to obtain a good round sum!

But I ought to have remembered her own sweet words:

> "Let nothing disturb thee;
> Let nothing affright thee;
> All passeth away;
> God only shall stay;
> Patience wins all.
> Who hath God needeth nothing,
> For God is his All."

THE ESCORIAL.

On leaving Avila I soon arrived at the Station, where travellers stop who wish to see the Escorial. As I had a letter of introduction to the Vice-President, Señor Don Dionisio Gonzalez, from one of the Canons at Avila, I made up my mind to visit this renowned building, hoping I might be able to collect a few dollars amongst the Professors, &c. My hopes were more than realized. The Vice-President received me with great kindness. But what was joy as well as surprise, when I was introduced to one of the Professors, named Dr. Braun, who was once a Professor in St. Mary's College, Oscott! We got friends immediately, so that I soon found myself at home. Dr. Braun was a German, and spoke English admirably. I believe he taught Greek and Hebrew. He most kindly collected six pounds for me amongst the students and professors. As the Vice-President invited me to stop a few days, I gladly accepted his hospitality, partly because he promised to give me "letters of introduction" to some of his friends in Madrid, and especially because I was so anxious not to lose the golden opportunity of inspecting a place which Spaniards proudly call, "*La Octava Maravilla del Mundo,*" the eighth wonder of the world. The Escorial was also an object of deep interest to me *then*, because I knew I should be able to see the original MS. of St. Teresa's "Life," in her own handwriting, as well as other MSS. The immense building in 1866 (when I was there) was full of life. By a Royal Decree of Her late Majesty Isabella II., dated August 5th, 1859, it was erected into a *seminary* for Ecclesiastical Students, as well as Secular. Her Majesty appointed her saintly Confessor, His Excellency Señor Don Antonio Maria Claret, as President, with a Vice-President and a staff of officials, consisting of a Rector, Vice-Rector, Chaplains, Librarian, Master of Ceremonies, Sacristans, and Professors for all branches of knowledge that are usually taught in Colleges and Universities.[*] It was a great success. More than *three hundred* persons inhabited the building: the strictest discipline was observed, and a fine Ecclesiastical spirit seemed to exist amongst the Church students. I had the great pleasure of being there on a Sunday. The Services were exceedingly grand and solemn. I assisted in the choir at Vespers, when the strains of the Gregorian plain chant were heard to perfection, at least as far as I could judge. The choral books (*Los libros de Coro*) are absolutely colossal, some of them being

[*] All these and other details are given by the President in a small volume which he gave me, entitled "Miscelanea Intcresante." (Barcelona, 1865.)

two yards wide : each leaf was made from the
skin of a calf! Several of them are gloriously
illuminated by Andres de Leon, and his pupil,
Ambrosio de Salazar. After Vespers the Vice-
President showed me the very stall which Philip
II. used to occupy whenever he assisted at Vespers or Mass. Here His Majesty was kneeling,
(I was told) absorbed in prayer, when through a
small door a messenger glided bearing the news
of the victory over the Turks at Lepanto. He
said nothing, nor did his countenance change,
but he continued his interrupted prayers : after
Vespers he communicated the joyful news to the
Prior, and ordered the *Te Deum* to be sung.

It would be out of place to give here a
lengthened description of the Escorial,* as it is
not connected directly with my subject. Many
books can be consulted about it, both in English
and in Spanish. Mr. Ford, in his "Handbook
for Travellers in Spain"—(part II. p. 749. Ed.
London, 1855,)—gives a long description of the
immense building, mixed, however, with a great
deal of matter which is irrelevant. His observations on Philip II. are especially objectionable.
He evidently did not understand the true character of that abused and maligned Monarch;
hence, when he calls him " a bigot—a despot—
" a suspicious tyrant—impersonation of Roman-
" ism," &c., he only panders to the ignorance and
prejudice of so many Englishmen, who like the

* Oftentimes spelt *Escurial;* there are authorities for both forms.

writers in the "Saturday Review," and other Periodicals, still call Queen Mary of England *bloody*, and Elizabeth "*the Virgin Queen*." Whatever may have been the faults and mistakes of Philip II., he was evidently a King of refined taste, a great Patron of the arts, and imbued with a deep religious spirit, and a zeal for the beauty of God's House, and the exaltation of the Catholic faith. But his life has yet to be written, for Mr. Prescott has shown him but scant justice.

Another account of the Escorial in English, which I prefer to Ford's, is given by Henry O'Shea, Esq., in his "Guide to Spain and "Portugal." (London: Longmans and Co., 1869, p. 128.)

Another book entitled "Rambles in Spain, in 1830," by Henry D. Inglis, is interesting, because he visited the Escorial when it was inhabited by a hundred monks of the Jeronymite Order; he was shown over the whole of the building by the Prior himself, Padre Buendia. But the writer is a thorough Protestant, for he tells us, how in approaching the Monastery the only sound he heard was that of the Convent bell. "But to me," (he adds) "there is nothing "poetic in a Convent bell: it only reminds me of "bigotry and ignorance, absurd penance, or sinful "hypocrisy!" (P. 274.)

A very excellent description will be found in Lady Louisa Tenison's magnificent work, entitled "Castile and Andalusia." (London, 1853, pp. 422, 423.)

Another account is given by Theophile Gautier, in his "Wanderings in Spain." (Chap. VIII., p. 103. London, 1853.)

In Spanish the two best works to consult are (1) " Historia de la Orden de San Geronymo," by José de Sigüenza, (4 vols., Madrid; 1st and 2nd parts appeared in 1590 : and the 3rd in 1605.) Sigüenza was the first Prior, and an eye-witness of its building, according to Ford. The other work (2) is by Padre Francisco de los Santos; it is entitled "Descripcion del Real Monasterio de San Lorenzo del Escorial." (Madrid, 1657.) I possess a copy of this valuable and scarce work, with plates, &c. A poor translation of it has appeared in English. (4to, London, 1671.) The best modern guide is "Descripcion Artistica, &c," by D. Bermejo. (Madrid, 1820.) There is a still more recent one by *Quevedo*, which I have not seen; it is entitled, "Historia del Real Monasterio de San Lorenzo," &c. (Madrid, 1849.) These and other Spanish writers agree in stating, that the "*first stone*" was laid with great solemnity, and in the presence of the King and all the principal nobles of the Court, on the 23rd of April, 1523, by Don Juan Bautista de Toledo. He died in 1567, and was succeeded by his pupil—Juan de Herrera* who made several

* He is not a favourite with some English Architects, especially with Mr. G. Edmund Street, who refused to visit the Escorial *because* it was built by Herrera !

happy alterations, though on the whole he seems to have followed the original design. He was ably assisted by Fray Antonia de Villacastin, who is buried in one of the Cloisters. The building advanced so rapidly, that it was completed in 1584, just 21 years after it had been begun, and at the then enormous cost of about £660,000. The common tradition that Philip built the Escorial on account of a vow which he had made at the time of the Battle of *St. Quentin*, gained over the French, August 10th, 1557, has been rejected by many modern critics on the ground that contemporary writers make no mention of the fact. But a document found a few years ago amongst the archives at Simancas leaves but little doubt on the matter, viz., that a vow was actually made. (See *Documentos Inéditos*. Tom. xxviii. P. 567.)

But other motives, also, no doubt influenced Philip. His Father, the Emperor Charles V., had ordered by his will that his body should remain at Yuste, until a more suitable place for his interment should be provided by his Son. Hence the Escorial was evidently intended to be a "Mausoleum" for the parents of Philip, as well as for the descendants of the Royal line of Austria, including at the same time two other objects—of being a Palace and a Monastery.

I may add that several "Letters" of St. Teresa are addressed to Philip II., for whom she appears always to have had a high esteem.* O! may she intercede for the welfare, both religious and political, of her beloved and noble land, now torn and distracted, and almost ruined by men whose sole ambition appears to be, to supplant each other by plots, intrigues, robbery, and a violation of the laws of God and the Church.

Charles V.† died on the 20th of September, 1558, in the most edifying sentiments of devotion and resignation. Archbishop Carranza, seeing that the Emperor's last hour had come, put into his hand a blest candle from our Lady's Shrine at Monserrate; and into his right hand the same crucifix which had been taken from the hand of his wife—who died at Toledo. For a few moments he devoutly contemplated the figure of his crucified Savour, and then clasping

---

* This good opinion which the Saint always seems to have had of this abused and mis-understood Sovereign, goes a great way in convincing us, that his character is not at all so bad as most English writers would fain make us believe. Don Vicente—in his Edition of the Saint's " Letters "— gives all those which she wrote to His Majesty, the originals of which still exist. In every one of them she speaks with the greatest respect and gratitude of His Majesty, for his constant kindness towards her, and the great interest he took in the work of the Reform. In her " *Book of the Foundations*," also, she thus mentions him by name :—" But the King now " reigning, Don Philip, was so good to me that on my writing to him he gave " orders for the issuing of the license, so ready is he to help those religious, " who, he knows, keep their Rule : for when he heard of our way of living in " these Monasteries, and of our observance of the primitive Rule, he helped us " in everything : and so I earnestly beg of you, my Daughters, always to make " special intercessions for His Majesty, as we are doing at present." (*Foundation of Caravaca*.)

† Fray Prudencio de Sandoval printed his *History of Charles V.* at Valladolid in folio. The first part appeared in 1604, and the second in 1606.

it to his bosom, he was heard by the attendants around him to say—as if answering to a call, "Ya, voy, Señor,"—"Now, Lord, I am going." His fingers soon relaxed their hold of the crucifix: a few moments of wrestling between the soul and body followed, after which, with his eyes fixed on the figure of our Lord, and with a voice loud enough to be heard outside the room, he exclaimed, "Ay, Jesus"—and expired. The small Church at Yuste was only intended to be a temporary resting-place for his body; for the Emperor in his will had expressed a wish to be laid beside the corpse of his beloved wife and parents, in the Royal vaults in the Cathedral of Granada, where already reposed the bodies of Ferdinand and Isabella. Philip II., however, considered he had a discretionary power to dispose of his Father's body as he should judge best. He, therefore, resolved that it should be removed to the Escorial, as soon as a plain vault could be completed. This was done on the 4th of February, 1574. The vault was situated in front of the High-altar. It contained other bodies besides those of Charles V. and his wife.

Philip III. not forgetting the wishes and intentions of his Father, commenced the present Pagan—but solemn—Mausoleum styled "*El Panteon*," which was completed in 1654. On the 16th of March, the same year, the dust of the Austrian Kings of Spain, and of their

Consorts who had continued the Royal line, was translated with great solemnity from the vault originally prepared by Philip II. to the Sepulchral Chamber of the "Panteon." There were seven coffins, borne in solemn procession by three Grandees and three Jeronymite Friars, around the Church; then at last they were taken down the long marble staircase to their final resting-place, and each was placed in its marble sarcophagus, amidst the light of countless tapers and golden lamps. Before the body of Charles V. was raised up to the niche destined for it, the coverings were removed to enable Philip IV. to gaze on the face of his illustrious ancestor. "The corpse was found," says Mr. Stirling, "to be quite entire; and even some sprigs of "sweet thyme folded in the winding-sheet, re- "tained, as the Friars averred, all their vernal "fragrance after the lapse of four score winters. "After looking for some minutes, in silence, at the "pale dead face of the hero of his line, the King "turned to Don Luis de Haro, Duke of Abrantes, "and said, '*Cuerpo honrado, Don Luis.*'* "'Very honoured, Señor,' replied the Minister: "words brief indeed, but very pregnant." ("Cloister Life of Charles V." P. 253. London, 1553.)

It is mentioned by Mr. Stirling that Mr. Beckford used to relate "how, when he was leaving "Madrid, Charles III., as a parting civility,

---

* Honoured body, *Don Luis.*

"desired to know what favour he would receive at
"his hands. The boon asked and granted was
"leave to see the face of Charles V. in order to test
"the fidelity of the portraits by Titian. The finest
"*portraits* of Charles, as well as his remains, were
"then still at the Escorial. The marble sarco-
"phagus being moved from its niche, and the lid
"raised, the lights of the *Pantheon* once more
"gleamed on the features of the dead Emperor.
"The pale brow and cheek, the slightly aquiline
"nose, the protruding lower jaw, the heavy
"Burgundian lips, and the sad and thoughtful
"expression, remained nearly as the Venetian
"had painted them, and unchanged since the
"eyelids had been closed by Quixada. There,
"too, were the sprigs of thyme seen by Philip
"IV., and gathered seven ages before in the
"woods of Yuste."* ("Cloister Life," &c.
P. 254.)

In a work† just published by Augustus J. C.
Hare, Esq., and entitled "Wanderings in Spain,"
the writer mentions the following fact in con-
nection with the account quoted above by Mr.
Stirling:—" Brantôme declares that the Inquisi-
"tion proposed that his body (the Emperor's)
"should be burnt for having given ear to heretical

---

* This account Mr. Stirling says he received from Mr. Beckford's *daughter*, the Duchess of Hamilton.

† This work, though here and there betraying Protestant ideas and prejudices, is, on the whole, very interesting. The plates are excellent. But the writer makes a sad mistake in stating (p. 251) that St. Teresa died at *Arila*, instead of Alba de Tormes—which he omitted to visit.

"opinions. It remains, however, though curi-
"osity—not heresy—has twice caused the coffin
"to be opened. The last time was in 1871, during
"the visit of the Emperor of Brazil, when hun-
"dreds of people flocked forth from Madrid to
"look upon the awful face of the mighty dead,
"which was entire even to the hair and eye-
"brows, though perfectly black." (P. 224. 2nd
Ed. London, 1873.)

Laus Deo Semper.

APPENDIX.

LETTER I.

To Señor Lorenzo de Cepeda y Ahumada.

[The letters which the Saint wrote to her Brother are very interesting. The date of this is 1561. It was written from Avila; it is the first in chronological order, though in most of the Spanish Editions, anterior to that of Don Vicente de la Fuente, it is numbered—*Carta* XXIX. He had lived for more than thirty-four years in South America, whence he had sent her some money, when she was engaged in founding St. Joseph's Convent at Avila. It came most opportunely, as she was then reduced almost to her last farthing.]

JESUS.—May the Holy Ghost ever dwell in your heart, and reward you for the care you have taken in coming so diligently to our assistance. I trust in God you will gain great merit by so charitable an act, for it is certain you bestow your charities just when they are wanted; and all those to whom you sent the money stood so much in need of it that you have given me great consolation. I believe God inspired you to send me so great a sum; for what I received from Juan Pedro de Espinosa and Varrona—(such I think is the name of the other merchant)—will be sufficient for my necessities for many years, especially for a poor little nun like myself, who considers it an honour, glory be to God, to wear a patched habit.

As I informed you a long time ago, I spent the money in a matter I could not avoid undertaking for several reasons, but chiefly for this one: because God had given me so many strong indications to commence this work, that is, to found a Monastery in which there are to be thirteen religious, and no more, who will be bound to live in strict enclosure, and will, therefore, never be allowed to go out. I dare not commit to writing in a letter everything of this nature. I can only tell you that learned and holy people assure me I must not play the coward, but do everything in my power for this undertaking. They will not be allowed to see any one, except with their veil down; their chief duty will be to devote themselves to prayer and mortification, as I have told you before at greater length. I will give you more information when Antonio Moran departs.

Señora Doña Yomar,* who writes to you, is of great service to me. She is the widow of Francisco de Avila, who belonged to the family of Sobralejo—if you remember. It is nine years since her husband died: he was a rich man. She now enjoys his property, besides the money which she has inherited from her own family: and although she was left a widow at the age of twenty-five, she has never married again, but given herself entirely to God. She is a very spiritual person. It is now more than four years since I contracted so close a friendship, that I now love her as if she were a sister of mine. But although she assisted me in the "Foundation," by giving me a good part of her income, she cannot now relieve me, because she now has no money. With regard to the purchase of the house, I must do this with ready money, by the Divine assistance. I have already received (though the Monastery has not yet commenced) the dowry for two Sisters. By the help of this sum I have secretly purchased the house, though I have not money enough to re-model it for a Monastery. But I have great confidence in God's assistance, knowing that it is His will the thing should be done. I have engaged the workmen, though it may have seemed very foolish to do so. But His Majesty took care of us all, and moved you to come to our assistance. What

* Or Guiomar, as it is spelt in all Editions. But the Saint seems to have pronounced and spelt the word as it is in the text. (De la Fuente.)

surprises me the more is, that I was so much in want of the
"forty crowns" * which you sent me, I think St. Joseph—
(after whom the Monastery is to be called)—helped me
through you. Though the house is poor and small, it has a
good prospect, and I think we shall have room enough.

Some of the Fathers have gone to Rome for the Bulls, for
though the house will belong to the Order, we shall have to
be under obedience to the Bishop. I trust in our Lord that
all things will prosper, for his greater glory, if we should
succeed in the undertaking—(as I think we certainly shall)—
because those who are to enter the house are chosen souls,
capable of becoming great examples of humility, penance,
and prayer. I beg of you to recommend the matter to God.
I hope, by the assistance of His grace, everything will be
finished before Antonio Moran goes away.

When he came here I received great comfort from him.
He seems to be a man on whom one can depend, and to
possess sound judgment. He gave me every particular
about you. I think that the greatest favour our Lord
could bestow upon me was to make me understand, from
what he told me, that you were convinced of the vanity of
the world, and had made a resolution to retire from it
altogether and live in quiet and repose. If you do so I am
certain you will be walking in the road to heaven: this was
what I wanted most to know, for till then I had been a little
uneasy about you. Glory be to him who doth all things
well. May He give you grace to advance more and more in
His service; for since the reward will be without bounds, we
ought not to make any delay in endeavouring to serve our
Lord, but each day strive to advance, however little it may
be, with such fervour that it may appear we are always at
war, as is indeed the truth; and that until we gain the
victory we desire to have no rest, nor to give way to any
negligence. All those with whom you sent the money were
men to be depended upon, though Antonio Moran has
excelled them all, both in selling the gold at a good price and

* Los quaranta pesos," &c.

also without any expense, as you will see, and also in having brought it here all the way to Madrid, to the prejudice of his health, for he was very unwell on the journey, though he is now better. I see that he is truly attached to you. He has brought Varrona's money, also, with great care. Rodriguez came with him likewise; he has done his duty well. I will send you a letter by him should he depart first. Antonio Moran has shown me the letter which you wrote to him. Be assured that the care you have taken of us is to my mind not only the effect of your goodness, but must have been inspired by God Himself.

My Sister Maria* yesterday sent me this letter. She will write to you again, as soon as she has received the rest of the money. It came just as it was wanted. She is a very good Christian, but full of troubles; and should Juan de Ovalle go to law against her, it will be the ruin of her children. The matter, however, is not so grievous as one might suppose, though it was certainly wrong to sell the property and destroy it. But Martin de Guzman may have had his reasons for so acting, and God forgive him. . The Court has decided in his favour—against all justice. I cannot endure that what my father sold (God rest his soul), should now be demanded back again. . . . . .

My Sister Juana† has married well. I assure you she is a very good woman, and very generous; she has the soul of an angel, praise be to God. I am the worst of all the family, whom you would hardly know to be your Sister, because I have degenerated so much: this I say in all sincerity. My Sister has had many troubles, but she has borne them with great patience. If you can send her anything, without injury to yourself, do so as soon as possible, even though it be a little at a time. You will see by this letter that the money has been delivered as you ordered. Toribia and her husband are dead; we distributed the money amongst her children, who are poor; and this has given them

* Doña Maria de Cepeda, who was married to Don Martin Guzman.
† Juana de Ahumada, wife of Juan de Ovalle.

great assistance. We also had all the Masses said which you wished. I think some had been said even before the money came. They were offered for the good intentions you named, which pleased me much, and edified me too. I had them by the best Priests I could find. In the midst of all this business I am now living in the house of Doña Yomar. I find great pleasure in being amongst persons who so frequently speak of you. I will tell you the occasion which procured me this happiness. As a daughter of this Lady, who is a Nun in our Monastery, was allowed to go and see her Mother, the Provincial ordered me to accompany her. Here I enjoy more liberty in everything I wish, than I did when I was at my Sister's house, because we speak of nothing but of God, and are very re-collected. I shall stay here till Father Provincial orders me to go elsewhere. I wish he would allow me to stop for some time, for here I am better able to manage the business about which I spoke to you.

But let us now speak of my dear Sister Juana* though I name her last, she does not hold the last place in my heart I assure you. I pray to God for her with the same affection as I do for you. I thank her a thousand times for the favour she has done me. All that I can do for her is, often to recommend her and her child to God. I have recommended him especially to that holy Friar, Peter of Alcantara, who promised to pray for him. He is that religious about whom I have already written to you. , I have also requested the *Theatins*,† and several other persons to pray for him, whose supplications I hope God will hear. May His Majesty be pleased to make him better than his parents: I do not mean that they are not good, but I wish him to be something more. Always inform me of the love and union in which you both live, which will give me such great pleasure.

* Juana de Fuentes y Guzman, the wife of her Brother Lorenzo de Cepeda.
† "*Los Teatinos*:" the Saint means the *Jesuit* Fathers, who in her time were called " Theatins," and were thus confounded with another Order instituted by the Bishop of Theate, many of whose rules bore some resemblance to those of the Society.

I have told you, that when Antonio Moran departs I will send you a copy of the "Executory letters," which I am told cannot be better: this I shall do with the greatest care. But if by any misfortune they should be lost, or anything happen to them, so that he could not deliver them, I will send you some others, until I hear you have received them safe. It is owing to the caprice of a certain person, whose name I do not wish to mention, that they have not been sent sooner. You will also receive some relics which I shall send you; they are enclosed in a case which has not cost much. I beg of God to keep you both in health for many years; to-morrow is the eve of the year 1562.

Having been engaged with Antonio Moran, I was obliged to commence writing when it was late; had not this been the case, I should have written a longer letter. But as he intends setting off to-morrow, I will keep the rest of the news till my Brother Jeronimo Cepeda goes away, and then I will send you a letter by him. But it is no matter, I have written in such haste. Always read my letters, I have taken care that the ink should be good. I have, however, written this letter in such a hurry and so late, as I told you, that I have had no time to read it over again. My health is better than it used to be. May God grant you such health of soul and body as I desire for you. Amen. I have no time to write to Señor Hernando de Ahumada, nor to Pedro de Ahumada; but I will do so soon. I desire to tell you that certain good people who are in our secret (I mean who know of this undertaking) consider it a miracle that you sent the money just at the time it was wanted. I hope in God that when I want any more He will move your heart to assist me, even should you be unwilling.

Your very sincere servant,*
DOÑA TERESA DE AHUMADA.†

* In the original, "*De Vuestra merced muy cierta Servidora.*"
† This signature the Saint always used before she founded St. Joseph's Monastery. When she was chosen Prioress of that house she assumed the sweet name of *Teresa de Jesus.*

LETTER II.

To Señor Lorenzo de Cepeda.

[This letter is not the next in chronological order, as it was written in 1570. In most other Spanish Editions it is numbered—*Carta* xxx.; but in Don Vicente's Edition it is annotated—*Carta* xviii. It was printed in previous Editions in a mutilated state, and very incorrect, until the Editor of the New Edition, referred to above, found a complete and corrected copy of it in the " Biblioteca Nacional," at Madrid. Palafox praises this letter as most valuable and interesting.]

JESUS.—May the Holy Spirit be always with you.

I wrote to you by four different ways, and by the third I sent a letter to Señor Jeronimo de Cepeda. As you must have received some of my letters, I will not answer all you said: neither will I say anything now respecting the good resolution with which our Lord has inspired you, and for which I praise His Majesty exceedingly. I certainly think you have done quite right, because I judge by the reasons which you mention that have induced you to take this resolution, there may be, more or less, other reasons also: I trust in our Lord that all may tend to His glory. In all our Monasteries we offer up continually especial prayers for you; and since it is your intention to serve God, may His Majesty direct everything for your good and the welfare of your children.

I have already informed you that six convents* have now been founded, and two houses for the Fathers of the Reform, in which they advance much in perfection: the houses of the Sisters are all established according to the model of St. Joseph's, at Avila, so that they seem to form but one and the same house; this gives me great consolation on beholding how truly our Lord is served in them, and with what purity of soul He is there loved and praised. At present I am residing in Toledo; and on the evening of the Annunciation

* The six were those of St. Joseph's, at Avila, Medina del Campo, Valladolid, Toledo, and Pastrana. The two houses of the Fathers were at Durvelo and Pastrana.

of our Lady I shall have been a year here, though I went to a town where Rui-Gomez lived, who is Prince of Eboli; there was founded a Monastery for Men and another for Nuns, both of which are going on well. I returned here to finish what remained to be done in this house, which promises to become one of our principal houses. I have had much better health this winter, because the air of this part of the country is so pure. If I did not see that it would be unfit for your children to reside here, I was thinking of inviting you to come and settle in Toledo, on account of the fineness of the climate. But there are several places around Avila where you could pass the winter, as several others do. With regard to my Brother Jeronimo de Cepeda, I think that when God brings him back to this country he will enjoy better health here. But may all be directed as His Majesty wills; I believe I have not had such good health for forty years as I have now, though I observe the rules like all the others do, and never eat meat except through great necessity,

About a year ago I had the quartan-ague; but it left me in better health than it found me. I was engaged in the Foundation at Valladolid, where I was almost killed by the kindness of Doña Maria de Mendoza, widow of the Secretary Cobos,* who has a great affection for me. Thus God gives us health when He sees it necessary for our good, but when not necessary He sends us sickness. May He be praised in all things. I was sorry to hear you had sore eyes, which are very painful to bear. Thank God they are now better.

Juan de Ovalle has already told you how he left here for Seville. One of my friends gave him such good directions, that on the very day he arrived there he drew the money. He has brought it here, and at the end of this month of January it will be distributed according to your wishes. In my presence was made out the amount of duty which is to be paid to the King. I have used no small diligence to gain some knowledge in these matters, and I have become such a

* He was a great favourite of Charles V., and Secretary of State under Philip II., who highly honoured and esteemed him.

woman of business, by means of these Foundations and other matters belonging to the Order, that I know a little of everything. And as I consider your affairs His business also, I am glad to have something to do with them. Lest I should forget, I must tell you that Cueto's son is dead ; he was quite young ; this happened since I last wrote to you ; you see nothing can be depended upon in this life ; every time I remember this I am consoled on reflecting how deeply convinced you are of this truth.

When I have finished the business which detains me here, I shall be glad to return to Avila, because as I am still the Prioress there I do not wish to offend the Bishop, to whom both myself and the whole Order are so much indebted. I know not how our Lord will dispose of me if I go to Salamanca, where a house has been offered me ; and though the journey is wearisome, yet the benefit which the people derive in all theto wns where these houses are established is so great that my conscience obliges me to found as many as possible ; our Lord, too, assists me in such a manner, that I am thereby animated to persevere.

I quite forgot to tell you in my other letters how many advantages and opportunities you would have in Avila, in order to bring up your children well. The Fathers of the Society * possess a College there, in which grammar is taught to the Students ; they go to confession every eight days, and become so virtuous that I am thereby excited to praise our Lord. Philosophy, and afterwards Theology, are taught in the College of St. Thomas,† thus without leaving the place every help can be found there requisite for the acquisition both of virtue and of learning. The people, too,

---

* "Tiénen los de Compañia un Colegio, á donde los enseñan gramática, y los confiesan de ocho á ocho dias, &c." The College was founded in 1553. The word *gramatica* may be translated by "Humanities," which includes grammar, classics, &c.

† This was founded in 1482, by Ferdinand and Isabella, at the request of the celebrated Inquisitor Fray Tomàs Torquemada. It is now almost in ruins, lying desolate outside the city, with its grass-grown cloisters. Some of the Saint's Dominican Confessors were Professors there.

are in general so devout* that those who come from other places are quite edified with them; great numbers are given to mental prayer and a frequenting of the Sacraments; even secular persons there lead a life of high perfection, amongst whom is the good Francisco Salcedo.† You have bestowed a great favour upon me, in sending Cepeda such a fine present; he cannot thank you sufficiently for it. He is truly a holy man; and in calling him such I only speak the truth. It is now a year since Pedro del Peso‡ died; he was very old, and his career was honourable. Ana de Cepeda is very grateful for the alms you sent her; with that she will be rich, for as she is so very good many other persons are kind to her. There are many places where she could live, but her state is so peculiar as to make her unfit for society. Still this is the way in which God leads her. But I could never venture to take her into any of our houses, not that she is deficient in virtue, but because I thought the state in which she now lives is better for her. I assure you, then, that she will not live with Doña Maria, nor with any one else; and this suits her purpose very well. Her life seems to resemble that of a hermit, and she possesses all the goodness and practises all the austerities of one. The son of Doña Maria, my sister, the wife of Martin de Guzma, has made his profession and makes great progress in virtue. I have already informed you of the death of Doña Beatrix, and that her daughter Doña Madalena, who was the youngest, is now a pensioner in a convent. I earnestly wish God would call her to be a religious; she is a very good young woman. It is now many years since I have seen her. At present her friends talk of marrying her to a widower, who is the oldest of the family, but I know not how the affair will end.

* They have the same devout character at the present day.
† St. Teresa thus speaks of him in her " Life " (chap. xxiii.)—"This " blessed and holy man seems to me, by the pains he took, to have been the " beginning of salvation to my soul, &c." After the death of his wife he became a Priest, and was Chaplain and Confessor to the Nuns of St. Joseph.
‡ A relation of St. Teresa, for her father's *first* wife was named Doña Catalina del Peso y Henao.

I believe I have also told you that the favour you bestowed on my Sister was done just at the time she stood in need of it. I have been quite astonished at all the troubles and inflictions our Lord has been pleased to send her, though she has borne them very patiently, and for this reason I believe our Lord now wishes to give her some relief. As for myself, I want nothing. I have more than is necessary; I shall, therefore, give my sister part of the alms you sent me, and the rest I shall spend in good works for your intention. I was, however, very glad to receive part of this money on account of certain scruples which I had, for in these Foundations many circumstances happen which require me to spend something, however careful I may be; and sometimes I spend all I have on these Foundations. Yet I know I might give less in certain cases, about which I consult learned men (to such I always mention the affairs of my soul), though no doubt I often consult them about mere trifles. The money you sent me was a great relief to me, for it spared me the unpleasantness of borrowing, though I am sure many would have assisted me. The world is so self-interested that for this very reason I have a horror of riches, and I am very glad I possess none.

People are so blind as to have a good opinion of me, and I know not the reason of it; but it seems that I stand so high in their esteem that they would lend me any sum of money, however great.* Hence at the very time I have the greatest aversion to money our Lord seems to wish to encumber me with it more than ever; and this is no little cross to me. May His Majesty be pleased that I may serve Him in everything, for all things will one day come to an end.

It will be a great pleasure for me to see you here, for I receive so little from everything in this world that our Lord will perhaps be pleased to grant me this comfort, that so we

---

* Literally:—" Y tanto el que yo tengo, para flarme mil y dos mil ducados," &c.

both unite together in labouring for His honour and glory and the good of souls. I am quite grieved to see so many lost, and these poor Indians cost me many tears. May our Lord enlighten them, for there and here there are many miseries. This I know too well; for as I visit many places, and speak with many persons, I cannot too often exclaim that we are worse than beasts because we know not the great dignity of our souls, which we debase by being attached to the things of this world. God grant us light.

I did not think of writing such a long letter, but I am anxious you should understand what a precious death your wife Señora Doña Juana died. All of us here have recommended her* to our Lord, and in all our Monasteries solemn services have been performed for her repose, so that I hope in God she no longer stands in need of our prayers. Try as much as possible to drive away this grief you must feel at her loss, and take care not to be in number of those who forget that there is another life which endures for ever, and who lament over those who begin to live, when they are delivered from the miseries of this life. Remember me most kindly to my brother Jéronimo de Cepeda; tell him he must consider this letter as written to himself. I am much pleased to hear that he is making arrangements to return here in a few years. I hope he will be able to bring the children with him. It would be much better to have them altogether, so that we may help each other and be one day united for ever in heaven.†

Your unworthy servant,
TERESA DE JESUS.

January 17th, MDLXX.

---

* Doña Juana de Puentes y Espinosa. St. Teresa had the highest opinion of the extraordinary virtues of this excellent lady, to whom she often alludes in her writings. Palafox styles her—" Doña Juana de Puentes " y *Guzman*," but Don Vicente proves this to be a mistake. (See his note in this letter.)

† Don Vicente has corrected, in the Spanish text, many mistakes made in preceding editions, and supplied several omissions from a MS. of this letter preserved in the *Biblioteca Nacional*.

Letter III.

To the Most Illustrious Lord Don Alvaro de Mendoza, Bishop of Avila.

[In one of the Saint's letters to her brother, Lorenzo de Cepeda, she mentions how she once heard a voice in the interior of the soul saying—*Buscate en mi*—"Seek thyself in me." She recommends him to correspond with the Divine call implied in these words. The Bishop, to whom this letter is addressed, having become acquainted with what the Saint heard, expressed a wish that the words should become the subject of a spiritual conference or recreation. Four persons were chosen to give their opinion on the meaning of the words; viz., St. John of the Cross, Father Julian de Avila, Francisco de Salcedo, and St. Teresa's brother. After these persons had each sent their explanations of the words to the Bishop, his Lordship sent the answers to the Saint, and commanded her, under obedience, to examine them and give her opinion on their correctness. This she playfully does in the present letter. Date, 1577.]

Jesus.—Did not obedience compel me I should not certainly have answered your Lordship's letter, nor should I have accepted the commission you gave me for certain reasons, though not for those which the Sisters allege. They say "that I refuse to pronounce who gave the best explanation "simply because my brother is amongst those whose explana- "tion is to be examined, and that my affection for him might "induce me to be partial in my judgment." But this is not the reason, because I love all equally, since all have assisted me in supporting my labours ; and my brother only came in when my troubles were drawing to an end, and I had nigh finished drinking the chalice of our Lord, though since that time he has had some share in those trials, and by God's favour he will share in some more. May He give me grace not to say any thing which might expose me to be denounced to the Inquisition ! My head still aches with all the affairs I have to attend to, and with the many letters which I have scribbled since last night. But obedience can do all things ; and therefore, whether well or ill, I shall endeavour to do what your Lordship commands. I thought I might have only a little amusement in reading these billets; but there is no remedy.

The words in question are, in my opinion, a motto of the "Spouse of our Souls," who says: "Seek thyself in Me." It is evident then, that Don Francisco de Salcedo is mistaken, in trying to prove that God is in all things, for we already know that He is in all things. He also speaks a great deal of the understanding and of union; but we know that where there is union, there the understanding does not work; and if it works not, how can it seek? The words of David—"I will hear what the Lord God will speak in me"—please me much, because peace in the powers of the soul, which the Prophet calls a "people," is highly to be esteemed. But I do not intend to speak of all that has been said. I will only remark that the explanation is not to the point, for the Spouse does not say—"*Let us hear,*" but "*Let us seek.*"

But what is worse than this, if he does not retract, I will have him denounced to the Inquisition—which is near at hand; for after having often said, "*These are the words of St. Paul*, and the *Holy Spirit*, he admits at last that all he had written was nonsense! Let him correct the mistake instantly—if not, he shall see the consequence.

Father Julian de Avila commenced well, but ended badly—and so he deserves no praise. He was not asked to explain, how light uncreated can unite itself with light created, but how *we should seek ourselves in God*; neither was he requested to tell us the feelings of a soul, when united with her Creator; and whether or no there is any difference between them. He also adds:—"When the soul is purified." I think that virtues and the purification of the soul are not sufficient here, because everything is *supernatural*, bestowed by God on whom He pleases; and if we could have any quality or disposition for such a gift—it is Love! But I pardon his mistakes, because he is not so prolix as my Father, John of the Cross. In his answer he lays down very sound doctrine, fit for those who wish to go through the

"Exercises" used by the Fathers of the *Society of Jesus*; but his explanation is not to the point in question.

It would cost us dear could we "seek" God only when we are dead to the world. Magdalen, the Samaritan and Cananæn women, were not so dead when they found Him. He likewise enters into many details as to how a soul, by means of union, becomes one and the same with God. But when He has bestowed this favour upon a soul He does not tell her "to seek Him," since she has already found Him. God preserve me from people who are so spiritual as to wish to make everything "perfect contemplation," without examining whence it comes. However, we are obliged to him for having given us such a good explanation of what we did not ask him about! But it is good always to be speaking about God, because thereby we derive much profit when we do not expect it.

With regard to Lorenzo de Cepeda, we are much obliged to him for his verses and his answer. But if he has said more than he understands, we forgive him on account of the amusement he has given us, and we pardon the little humility he has shown in attempting to explain such sublime things, as he acknowledges in his answer he does. And because he undertakes, without having been desired, to advise souls to aim at the "Prayer of Quiet" (as if it depended upon them); he already feels the pain of those who act in this manner. God grant that he may derive some profit from his connexion with such spiritual persons. His remarks have, however, given me great comfort, though I see he has many reasons to be ashamed of them. But I cannot decide whose remarks are the best, because it may be said, without injustice to any one, that all the four have fallen into mistakes.

I trust your Lordship will command those persons to correct themselves. Perhaps I should correct myself, by trying not to resemble my brother in his want of humility. All these gentlemen are so highly spiritual that they have failed only through having written too much, because (as I have already remarked) he who shall obtain the favour of having his soul united with God will have no further need "to seek Him," since he already possesses Him. I thank your Lordship again and again for your goodness in having written to me. But I shall write no more at present, lest I tire your Lordship with my nonsense.

Your Lordship's unworthy servant and subject,

TERESA DE JESUS.

These three "Letters" will, perhaps, give my readers some imperfect idea of the Saint's inimitable style. But it is almost impossible for any translation to do justice to the original. All the French translations are too diffuse, resembling more a paraphrase than an imitation of the *terseness* of the Spanish. Even the translation* by the Rev. Père Bouix, S.J., though so much superior in many respects to the preceding French versions, is blamed by Don Vicente de la Fuente," as being so free that Spaniards in reading it would hardly recognise St. Teresa.†

When shall we have a good translation of all the Saint's ." Letters " into English ? They are a perfect storehouse of spirituality ; and withal exceedingly witty, lively, and even jocose, thus proving that the " Saint of common sense " was *cheerfulness* itself, in the midst of her numerous trials and afflictions. With all her raptures, is it not also evident that she was a consummate " woman of business," as she styles herself ? Her solidity of judgment, her prudence, patience, and sweetness of disposition won the admiration of every one. It is quite unnecessary to quote here the high praise bestowed upon these " Letters " by Ribera, Yepes, Abbé Boucher, Bouix, Villefore, S. Antonio,‡ Palafox, Dom

* "Lettres de Sainte Térèse, traduites suivant l'ordre chronologique," &c., par Le Père Bouix, S.J. (Paris, 1861.)

† " Honra al traductor, aunque por altra parte la version es tan libre, que los Españoles apenas vemos en ella à Santa Teresa." (*Preliminares*, xxxviii.)

‡ " Giocondissima ella è la lezione di esse. Vi si scorge l'anima generosa di Teresa, una mente fra tanti travagli, infermità e affari, sempre limpida e vivace." (*Vita di Santa Teresa*. Tom iv., p. 454. Roma, 1837.)

Taste, Pelicot, Madame de Maupeou, Chappe de Ligni, the Bollandists, &c. Had the Saint left us nothing but her "Letters," these alone would have been sufficient to entitle her to our admiration, and to the gratitude of the scholar, the historian, and every devout soul in the world. It will be seen from the "Letters," that the Saint *always* spelt her name Teresa, and not "*Th*eresa" which comes from the French. Hence Père Bouix remarks, " Nous avons restitué " au nom de Térèse sa veritable orthographe. La Sáinte ainsi " que ses autographes le démontrent, n'a jamais mis d' *h* dans " son nom ; ses historiens l'ont écrit comme elle ; tous les " auteurs Espagnols ont fait de méme." (Avertissement du Traducteur.)

In conclusion I cannot omit quoting a passage from the Preface to the Translation of St. Teresa's "*Exclamations*," &c., by the illustrious Bishop Milner :—" I will " venture to assert that, so far as we can pronounce on the " opinion of the Church, where no formal decision has taken " place, there are perhaps no writings that have been more " pointedly or more strongly approved of by this unerring " Judge, than those of St. Teresa. Her Spirit of Prayer, " and the character of her ascetical works, were not only " examined and approved of by the most eminent Divines " of the age, but also by a constellation of her holy " contemporaries, such as St. Francis Borgia, St. Peter of " Alcantara, St. John of the Cross, St. Lewis Bertrand, &c., " who were the best because they were *experimental* judges " of the excellency of her ' *heavenly doctrine* ; ' for so it is " stated by the Church, as I observed before, in the Prayer " inserted in her public Liturgy, after a *second* examination " of our Saint's spirit and writings had taken place," &c. (P. 17. London, 1790.)

A LIST OF TRANSLATIONS ALREADY PUBLISHED

BY

THE REV. CANON DALTON.

1. "THE LIFE OF ST. TERESA," written by Herself.
   (2nd Edition, London, 1855.)
2. "BOOK OF THE FOUNDATIONS." . . . (1860.)
3. "THE WAY OF PERFECTION." . . . (1860.)
4. "CONCEPTIONS OF DIVINE LOVE." . . (1860.)
5. "THE MANSIONS, OR INTERIOR CASTLE." . . (1859.)
6. "LETTERS OF ST. TERESA." (Vol. 1) . . (1860.)
7. "A GRADUAL TO ASCEND UNTO GOD FROM THE CONTEMPLATION OF CREATED OBJECTS," by the Ven. Cardinal Bellarmine. . . . (London, 1844.)
8. "THE ART OF DYING WELL," by Cardinal Bellarmine.
   (Richardson and Son, Derby, 1846.)
9. "THE ETERNAL HAPPINESS OF THE SAINTS," by Cardinal Bellarmine. . . . . . (Richardson, 1848.)
10. "CATECHISM OF AN INTERIOR LIFE," by M. Olier.
    (Richardson, 1849.)
11. "A LITTLE BOOK OF THE LOVE OF GOD," by Count Stolberg, from the German . . (Burns, 1849.)
12. "THE SPIRIT OF ST. JOHN OF THE CROSS." (Richardson.)
13. "THE LIFE OF CARDINAL XIMENEZ," by Dr. Hefele, translated from the German, 8vo. . (London, 1860.)
14. "LIFE OF ST. WINIFREDE." . . (London, 1857.)

NOTE.

I particularly wish all my readers to remember, that the PROCEEDS *arising from the sale of this Narrative are to be given for a most charitable object.*

www.ingramcontent.com/pod-product-compliance
Lightning Source LLC
Chambersburg PA
CBHW020900160426
43192CB00007B/1016